STERLING BIO

MALCOLM X

A Revolutionary Voice

Beatrice **Gormley**

STERLING

New York / London
www.sterlingpublishing.com/kids

STERLING and the distinctive Sterling logo are registered trademarks of
Sterling Publishing Co., Inc.

Library of Congress Cataloging-in-Publication Data
Gormley, Beatrice.
  Malcolm X : a revolutionary voice for African Americans / Beatrice Gormley.
     p. cm. -- (Sterling biographies)
  Includes bibliographical references.
  ISBN-13: 978-1-4027-4589-8
  ISBN-10: 1-4027-4589-3
  1. X, Malcolm, 1925-1965--Juvenile literature. 2. Black Muslims--Biography--Juvenile litera-
ture. 3. African Americans--Biography--Juvenile literature. I. Title.
  BP223.Z8L5739 2007
  320.54'6092--dc22
  [B]
                                        2007019346

10 9 8 7 6 5 4 3 2 1

Published by Sterling Publishing Co., Inc.
387 Park Avenue South, New York, NY 10016
© 2008 by Beatrice Gormley
Distributed in Canada by Sterling Publishing
c/o Canadian Manda Group, 165 Dufferin Street
Toronto, Ontario, Canada M6K 3H6
Distributed in the United Kingdom by GMC Distribution Services
Castle Place, 166 High Street, Lewes, East Sussex, England BN7 1XU
Distributed in Australia by Capricorn Link (Australia) Pty. Ltd.
P.O. Box 704, Windsor, NSW 2756, Australia

Printed in China

Sterling ISBN-13: 978-1-4027-4589-8 (paperback)
        ISBN-10: 1-4027-4589-3

Sterling ISBN-13: 978-1-4027-5801-0 (hardcover)
        ISBN-10: 1-4027-5801-4

Designed by Catie Myers-Wood for Simonsays Design!

Image research by Larry Schwartz

For information about custom editions, special sales, premium and
corporate purchases, please contact Sterling Special Sales
Department at 800-805-5489 or specialsales@sterlingpublishing.com.

Contents

Events in the Life of Malcolm X

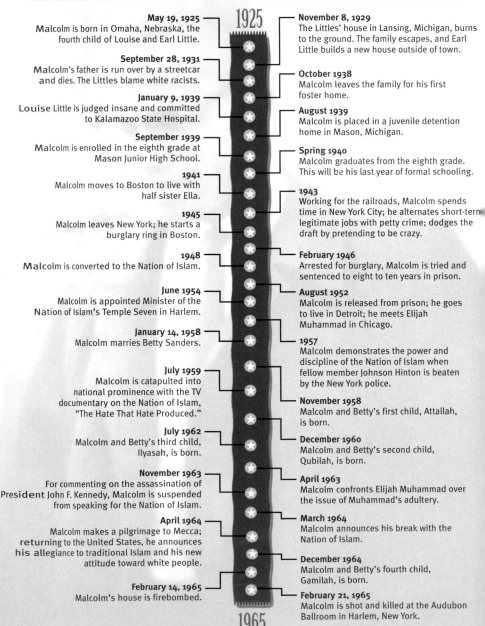

1925

May 19, 1925
Malcolm is born in Omaha, Nebraska, the fourth child of Louise and Earl Little.

November 8, 1929
The Littles' house in Lansing, Michigan, burns to the ground. The family escapes, and Earl Little builds a new house outside of town.

September 28, 1931
Malcolm's father is run over by a streetcar and dies. The Littles blame white racists.

October 1938
Malcolm leaves the family for his first foster home.

January 9, 1939
Louise Little is judged insane and committed to Kalamazoo State Hospital.

August 1939
Malcolm is placed in a juvenile detention home in Mason, Michigan.

September 1939
Malcolm is enrolled in the eighth grade at Mason Junior High School.

Spring 1940
Malcolm graduates from the eighth grade. This will be his last year of formal schooling.

1941
Malcolm moves to Boston to live with half sister Ella.

1943
Working for the railroads, Malcolm spends time in New York City; he alternates short-term legitimate jobs with petty crime; dodges the draft by pretending to be crazy.

1945
Malcolm leaves New York; he starts a burglary ring in Boston.

February 1946
Arrested for burglary, Malcolm is tried and sentenced to eight to ten years in prison.

1948
Malcolm is converted to the Nation of Islam.

August 1952
Malcolm is released from prison; he goes to live in Detroit; he meets Elijah Muhammad in Chicago.

June 1954
Malcolm is appointed Minister of the Nation of Islam's Temple Seven in Harlem.

1957
Malcolm demonstrates the power and discipline of the Nation of Islam when fellow member Johnson Hinton is beaten by the New York police.

January 14, 1958
Malcolm marries Betty Sanders.

November 1958
Malcolm and Betty's first child, Attallah, is born.

July 1959
Malcolm is catapulted into national prominence with the TV documentary on the Nation of Islam, "The Hate That Hate Produced."

December 1960
Malcolm and Betty's second child, Qubilah, is born.

July 1962
Malcolm and Betty's third child, Ilyasah, is born.

April 1963
Malcolm confronts Elijah Muhammad over the issue of Muhammad's adultery.

November 1963
For commenting on the assassination of President John F. Kennedy, Malcolm is suspended from speaking for the Nation of Islam.

March 1964
Malcolm announces his break with the Nation of Islam.

April 1964
Malcolm makes a pilgrimage to Mecca; returning to the United States, he announces his allegiance to traditional Islam and his new attitude toward white people.

December 1964
Malcolm and Betty's fourth child, Gamilah, is born.

February 14, 1965
Malcolm's house is firebombed.

February 21, 1965
Malcolm is shot and killed at the Audubon Ballroom in Harlem, New York.

1965

Truth in Black and White

What is looked upon as an American dream for white people has long been an American nightmare for black people.

Late one night in 1929, in Lansing, Michigan, four-year-old Malcolm Little woke up to smoke, flames, and screams. The house was on fire. Malcolm's father and mother rushed their confused and terrified children, including a new baby, out of the burning house. They stood shivering in their underwear as the house burned to the ground.

When Malcolm was older, he was told that white men had burned the Littles' house. The men were members of the Black Legion, a white **supremacist** group like the Ku Klux Klan that hated black people.

Such terrifying moments as these, as well as years of daily racist insults and barriers, shaped and transformed Malcolm Little. He grew up to become Malcolm X, leader of a **black nationalist** group. A powerful speaker, he dared to voice his frightening observations about race problems in America. For that reason many people, black and white, feared and even hated him. For the same reason, many people saw him as a hero—someone who was unafraid to speak the truth as he saw it, and was willing to stand up and fight for black equality and power.

CHAPTER 1

A Move to the North

I had learned that if you want something, you had better make some noise.

The life and attitudes of Malcolm X can be traced back to his humble beginnings and to the beliefs that his father and mother held about black pride and black independence in America.

Malcolm's father, Earl Little, grew up on a farm in Georgia. His family was poor, but they were better off than many black southerners of that era, because they owned the land they farmed. Like many of his family and neighbors, Earl dropped out of school after the third or fourth grade. He married and had three children, but he and his first wife separated.

For most African Americans living in the South, life was made harder by the unfair practices of the Jim Crow laws that kept black people separated from white people in public places and establishments. Hoping, like thousands of other black southerners, to find a better way of life, Earl joined the migration north and moved to Montreal, Canada. There he met Louise Norton, a tall, slender girl with beautiful black hair down to her waist. They were married around 1919.

Louise had grown up in Grenada, an island nation in the Caribbean Sea. Her mother had died when she was young, and she knew nothing of her father except that he

Jim Crow Laws

Under the Jim Crow laws passed in the South soon after the Civil War, black people were not much better off than their enslaved ancestors. These state and local laws required that whites and blacks be **segregated** in all public facilities. Black children and white children could not attend the same public schools. Trains and buses had to provide separate seating for the two races. Blacks and whites had to use separate public drinking fountains and restrooms. Supposedly, these public facilities were "separate but equal." In fact, the facilities for African Americans were always worse than those for whites. Sometimes they were nonexistent.

"Separate but equal" facilities for blacks and whites were a common sight in the South. In this 1938 photograph, a black child uses the "colored" drinking fountain on the county courthouse lawn in Halifax, North Carolina.

was a red-haired white man. Unlike Earl, Louise had gone to school for several years, and she was proud that she spoke proper English and used correct grammar and pronunciation.

Followers of Marcus Garvey

One thing Earl and Louise shared was a devotion to Marcus Garvey, a black man from Jamaica. Garvey preached that the black race was actually superior to the white race—not inferior as most white Americans believed during the 1920s.

Garvey founded the Universal Negro Improvement Association (UNIA) to promote his ideas. He urged blacks to become independent from whites by starting their own businesses and doing business only with each other. He felt that eventually, blacks should return to Africa and form an independent nation there.

Marcus Garvey, photographed c. 1924, at his desk. Garvey gave many African Americans, including Malcolm's parents, pride in their race.

Many blacks thought that Garvey would only stir up trouble for them. They feared that Garvey's ideas would anger whites, who would take out their anger on all black people. Besides, they thought the idea of returning to Africa was ridiculous. Like white Americans, African Americans had the impression that black Africans were uneducated tribal people living in a jungle. Most black Americans at that time had no idea of the civilizations that had flourished in Africa throughout history.

Other African Americans, including Malcolm's mother and father, were inspired by Garvey's words: "To be a Negro is no disgrace, but an honor, and we of the Universal Negro Improvement Association do not want to become white." Earl led public meetings of the local UNIA, while Louise helped with the bookkeeping and wrote articles for the organization. Earl and Louise had good reason to think, as Garvey did, that black people could never live peacefully with white people. Just in Earl's family alone, three of his six brothers had been killed by white men.

On the Move

The Littles moved several times while their family was growing. Their first child, Wilfred, was born in Philadelphia. Hilda and Philbert were born in Omaha, Nebraska. The Littles were still in Omaha early in 1925, when Louise was pregnant with Malcolm. One night while Earl was away, the Ku Klux Klan came to the Littles' house. The Klansmen were after Earl, to punish him for spreading Marcus Garvey's ideas. When they found out that he wasn't home, they smashed the windows with their rifle butts. After Malcolm was born on May 19, Earl moved his family from Nebraska to Wisconsin. In 1929, they moved to Lansing, Michigan.

Life in the North turned out to be difficult for Earl and Louise, as it was for many African Americans from the South. Earl scraped out a living with carpentry jobs and as a visiting preacher. Factories such as the Oldsmobile plant in Lansing, Michigan, would not hire African Americans. Whites made it

African American boys, living in northern ghettos without parks or playgrounds, play on a city street in this photograph from c. 1925.

almost impossible for blacks to buy or rent homes in middle-class white neighborhoods. Most black migrants from the South found themselves barred from decent jobs and living in **ghettos** in the worst sections of the cities.

In Lansing, Earl resumed his volunteer work for the UNIA. Less than a year later, in November 1929, white racists burned the Littles' house down.

The Ku Klux Klan

After the Civil War, some embittered southerners reacted to **Reconstruction** by forming secret societies. The Ku Klux Klan was the best known of these. Riding out at night dressed in white sheets and hoods, they terrorized the newly freed blacks. The Klan's aim was to prevent black citizens from voting, getting an education, or running a business.

If blacks tried to assert their rights, the Klan resorted to violence. They burned homes, schools, and churches. They beat and sometimes killed black people who dared to defy them. Any whites who tried to help African Americans could expect the same treatment.

In the 1920s, the Ku Klux Klan was especially powerful. Today, although there are still Klan groups in the United States, they are small in number and are considered extreme, fringe organizations.

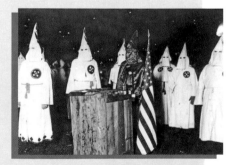

Robed Ku Klux Klan members were photographed c. 1920 around their altar during a midnight ceremony. This meeting drew 30,000 Klan members from Chicago and northern Illinois.

Earl and Louise decided their family would be better off outside the town. They bought a few acres of land on the outskirts of East Lansing, where Earl built the family a new house. They could be more independent here, because they could grow their own vegetables and raise chickens and rabbits on the land they owned. The house didn't have indoor plumbing, and it wasn't insulated against the cold Michigan winters, but it was as good as many of the houses in the area.

Young Malcolm begged to have his own vegetable plot, which he planted and weeded carefully. He was proud when the family ate *his* beans or corn for supper. He also liked the peacefulness of the garden, where he sometimes lay between the rows and gazed at the sky.

Malcolm's Early Impressions

Earl worked at short-term construction jobs, but mainly he earned his living as a traveling Baptist preacher. Malcolm and the rest of the family often went to one church or another to hear their father's sermons. Malcolm's brother Philbert loved church. He enthusiastically joined in as the congregation sang, jumped, and shouted responses to his father's preaching. Malcolm only sat staring, wondering how they could get so worked up. "I had very little respect for most people who represented religion," he said.

During the week, Malcolm's father also spoke at meetings of the UNIA. Sometimes he took Malcolm along with him. The meetings were held in members' living rooms, often in the daytime, because in many towns, black people weren't allowed on the streets after dark. This was true not only in East Lansing but also across the United States, north as well as south.

Malcolm enjoyed these black nationalism meetings much more than he did the church services. He was proud to hear his father, a tall, very dark man, speak of how black people could gain freedom, independence, and self-respect. He thrilled to Marcus Garvey's words: "Up, you mighty race, you can accomplish what you will!"

Malcolm was deeply impressed with the photographs of Marcus Garvey that his father showed at the meetings. Here was a *black* man in a splendid gold-trimmed uniform and plumed hat,

A follower of Marcus Garvey stands outside a Garvey club in New York in this photo from 1943. Garvey was forced to leave the United States in 1927, but his influence on black movements continued.

leading a parade through New York City! Malcolm also liked the way black people behaved at the UNIA meetings—intelligent and serious.

A Harsh Family Life

Earl and Louise Little had seven children in all. After Malcolm came Reginald, Yvonne, and Wesley. The Little children noticed that while their father was dark-skinned, their mother was so light-skinned that she could have passed for white. Philbert had the darkest skin of any of the children, and Malcolm had the lightest skin, as well as eyes of changeable color and light reddish hair.

Louise took pride in running the household, and she worked hard at cooking, cleaning, and washing and ironing clothes. Determined that her children would have a proper education, she urged them to do well in school. She supervised their homework, which they did at the kitchen table. If they mispronounced a word, Louise had them look it up in a dictionary.

But the Littles' family life was not always peaceful. Malcolm's brothers and sisters teased him for not looking like the rest of them. Malcolm and his brother Philbert fought. Also, their parents often quarreled bitterly. Sometimes Earl would even hit Louise.

Earl and Louise Little both punished their children harshly, too. Malcolm felt that his father beat him less and favored him over his brothers and sisters because Malcolm's skin was lighter. However, he was also convinced that his mother beat him more than the other children for the same reason. She often made remarks to the effect that he wasn't dark enough. After Malcolm grew up, he thought that his mother must have been very angry at her white father and ashamed that he never acknowledged her.

Malcolm's brothers and sisters teased him for not looking like the rest of them.

Young Malcolm didn't take his beatings quietly. He quickly learned to yell at the top of his lungs when he was punished, because his mother was embarrassed to have the neighbors hear him. He also learned to make a fuss when he wanted something, such as a buttered biscuit. His mother might scold him more than she did the others, but he got his biscuit. "So early in life," said Malcolm afterward, "I had learned that if you want something, you had better make some noise."

Malcolm started kindergarten in the fall of 1931. He and his brothers and his sister Hilda were the only black children in the school. Because the school was outside the city limits, the rules about segregated education were more relaxed. Also, because there were no other black children in the district, the white residents didn't see them as a threat. Therefore, the Little children were allowed to attend the white school.

Years later, Malcolm explained that the white teachers and students looked upon him and his brothers and sister as mascots, or symbols. The white boys and girls called the Little children "nigger" or "darkie." At the time, Malcolm didn't understand these **racist** names to be insults.

A Father's Death

Because of Earl Little's leadership in the UNIA, he made many enemies, black as well as white. White people were angry and afraid that he would "stir up" the African Americans of Lansing to demand better treatment. Blacks were afraid that because Earl spoke out against the injustices they suffered, the whites would punish all of them.

By the time Malcolm was six, the Black Legion, the white group that had burned down their first house in Lansing, was threatening his father again. One day, Malcolm's father and mother quarreled just before Earl left for town on an errand. But then Louise had an overwhelming feeling that something bad was going to happen. She cried a warning after him: "Early! Early! If you go, you won't come back!"

Louise was right. Earl didn't return for supper on the night of September 28, 1931. Late that night, the police came to the house, and Malcolm woke again to his mother's screams. Earl Little had been found on the streetcar tracks in Lansing, badly hurt. He was taken to the hospital, but he died before his wife reached him.

Later, Malcolm was told that his father's head had been bashed in before he was put on the tracks to be run over. The

Malcolm's father was found fatally injured on streetcar tracks similar to these, photographed in 1928.

official ruling was that his death had been accidental, that Earl had been drunk and had fallen under a streetcar. The family, however, was sure that white racists had murdered him. In any case, Louise Little was left alone with seven children to support.

Malcolm's father had two life insurance policies, but the main insurance company refused to pay. Although Earl's death had officially been declared "accidental," the company insisted that it had been a suicide. The policy stated that in case of suicide, the insurance company would not have to pay.

There was no evidence to suggest suicide, and Earl Little's family and friends were sure the insurance company ruling was only an excuse to cheat the family out of money. As Malcolm said later, "How could my father bash himself in the head, then get down across the streetcar tracks to be run over?"

CHAPTER 2

A Family Destroyed

Our family was so poor that we would eat the hole out of a doughnut.

Now the Little family consisted of seven young children and one parent—Louise—with no means of making a decent living. Sometimes Louise managed to get a job in town, cleaning and sewing for a white family, while Hilda minded her youngest brothers and sister. Most white people in Lansing didn't trust black people to work in their homes, but Louise was so light-skinned that she could be taken for white.

Sooner or later, though, Louise's employers would find out that she was not only black, but also the widow of that black nationalist Earl Little. Then they would fire her. When this happened, Louise would come home trying to hide her tears from her children. The sight would haunt Malcolm for the rest of his life.

Hard Times

It was 1931 when Malcolm's father died, and the country was already sliding into an economic slump called the Great Depression. The Littles grew poorer and poorer. As Malcolm said later, "Our family was so poor that we would eat the hole out of a doughnut."

Wilfred, the oldest boy in the Little family, quit school to work at odd jobs. This must have hurt Louise, who wanted so much for her children to be educated. But the

During the Great Depression, men waiting in breadlines, like the one shown, were a common sight in America. This c. 1930–34 photograph was taken at a charity center in New York.

Littles needed every penny Wilfred could earn. Malcolm and the younger children tried to help out, too. They hunted rabbits and frogs and sold the meat to white families. They walked the two miles to a bakery in Lansing, where they could buy a whole sack of day-old bread and cookies for five cents. The stale bread might be all that the children had for their school lunch the next day. Malcolm ate his lunch apart from his classmates, so that no one would see there was nothing between his two slices of bread.

Louise Little worked harder than ever to keep the family going. She kept on scrubbing the house and washing and ironing the children's threadbare clothes. She cooked bread pudding, meat loaf that was mostly bread, and other inventive recipes to stretch the little money she had. But often there wasn't even a nickel for a sack of stale bread, and the family's only dinner was a pot of boiled dandelion greens, picked from their yard.

Louise began to buy food and other necessities on credit, promising to pay later. As paying jobs became harder to find, her debts mounted up. Finally, she had to apply to the state **welfare agency** for help. It was either that or let her children starve.

The Great Depression

The Great Depression was a period in history when the economy of the United States took a sharp downturn. On October 29, 1929, the stock market on Wall Street in New York City crashed, causing banks to fail across the country—as Americans rushed to withdraw their money—and factories and businesses to collapse. American farmers, who were already suffering from plunging farm prices, fell on hard times. The Great Depression settled over the country like a blight.

Within a few years, thirteen million Americans were out of work. A severe drought swept the Great Plains, ruining crops for thousands of small farm owners in the central part of the United States. Despite the efforts of President Franklin D. Roosevelt's New Deal—government projects established to help Americans earn a living—the Depression lasted throughout the 1930s.

There was massive unemployment during the Great Depression. An unemployed man, photographed in 1935, leans hopelessly against the wall of an out-of-business coffee shop.

Going on Welfare

The Littles had always been scornful of families on welfare who received money and food from the state government. How could anyone be independent and self-respecting, as Marcus Garvey urged, if he or she accepted handouts from the government? Besides, welfare help didn't amount to much.

Like this washerwoman, photographed in Jackson, Mississippi, c. 1930–35, Louise Little washed clothes in Lansing for white people—when they would hire her.

A family of four received sixty cents a week, plus packages of government surplus food. But the Littles desperately needed the small amount of cash and the food. Now the Littles were one of those welfare families they had looked down on.

Most families on welfare hated the county commissioner—the official in charge of the local welfare agency. He seemed to enjoy making the clients feel like second-class citizens.

Some of the social workers who visited the Littles were sympathetic, but Louise couldn't tolerate what she felt was interference with her family. With her perfect diction and grammar, Louise let the social workers know that she was better educated than they were. Although the social workers sometimes had good advice, Louise's pride wouldn't let her accept it. For instance, they kept urging Louise to get her broken stove repaired instead of her car. However, owning a car—even an old, beat-up car—was a status symbol during the Depression. Louise couldn't bear to give it up.

Louise also refused a neighbor's offer of some pork, because she believed that pork was unclean food. Besides, she had just joined the Seventh Day Adventist Church, and this church did not allow its members to eat pork. From the welfare agency's point of view, the Littles were too poor to turn down any food, even food that didn't fit into their beliefs.

Above all, Louise hated any advice that suggested she wasn't able to take care of her children.

Above all, Louise hated any advice that suggested she wasn't able to take care of her children. Malcolm was often the cause of these suggestions, because he had started to steal. He would "lift" a snack for himself from a display of fruits outside a grocery store. His mother would whip him when she found out, and Malcolm, who was now just as tall as she, did not try to fight back. However, he kept right on stealing. He and his brother Philbert also fought constantly, and Louise couldn't make them stop.

Under the terrible strain of poverty and the struggle to keep the family going, Louise Little began to show some signs of mental illness. She stopped cooking and cleaning. For long periods of time, she ignored the children, talking only to herself. Hilda, the oldest daughter, kept the house as well as she could, but it was always dirty and messy.

Although Malcolm was obviously bright and had received good grades when he was younger, he was now getting into trouble at school. Even though he still loved to read, his grades were slipping, and he disobeyed his teachers. Malcolm, now thirteen, was expelled from his junior high school for misbehavior in the fall of 1938 and was transferred to another school.

Placed in a Foster Home

At the same time, the state welfare agency placed Malcolm in a **foster home** with a black family, the Gohannas, near his new school. By this time, Louise Little had lost her fighting spirit, and she didn't try to stop Malcolm from being taken away. Malcolm already knew the Gohannas and liked them. Still, he had mixed feelings about leaving his own family—even though his family was falling apart.

Malcolm left his home and family for a new, temporary home. His mother grew more and more disconnected from reality until she had a complete mental breakdown. At the beginning of 1939, she was committed to the Kalamazoo State Hospital in Kalamazoo, Michigan. Wilfred and Hilda were old enough to stay on in the Littles' house by themselves, but the other children were placed in different foster homes.

Later in life, Malcolm blamed the welfare agency for breaking up the Little family. He thought that the social workers, with their constant interference, were somewhat responsible for causing his mother's mental illness. He felt that they had turned the children against each other and had persuaded Malcolm that he would be better off in a foster home.

This photo shows the Kalamazoo State Mental Hospital, where Louise Little lived for more than twenty-four years. In 1963, she was released and went to live with Malcolm's brother Philbert.

At the time, Malcolm was relieved to be living with the Gohannas, where at least there was always enough to eat. They were an older couple, and their only other child at home was Big Boy, a nephew about Malcolm's age. That fall, 1938, Malcolm and Big Boy attended West Junior High School, a mostly black school in Lansing.

An Angry Boy

Inspired by the African American boxing champion of that era, Joe Louis, Malcolm's brother Philbert started entering boxing competitions and did fairly well. Malcolm tried to copy his brother's success. As he said later, the boxing ring was "the only place a Negro could whip a white man and not be **lynched**." Despite being big for his age, Malcolm turned out to be a poor boxer. In fact, he was soundly beaten by his first opponent, a white boy. Malcolm trained hard, determined to do better. Then he asked for a rematch, but the same white boy knocked him out in the first round. Malcolm gave up boxing after his defeat, feeling like a complete failure. His family was shattered, he was doing poorly in school, and he couldn't out-box that white boy, no matter how hard he tried. His shame turned to anger, and his pent-up anger ate at him.

Soon after his humiliating boxing bout, Malcolm walked into his classroom with his hat on—which was against the school rules. The white teacher knew Malcolm was breaking the rule on purpose. Trying to make Malcolm look foolish, he ordered him to walk around and around the classroom while the lesson went on. As he obeyed the order, Malcolm waited until the teacher had his back turned. Then he placed a tack upside down on the seat of the teacher's chair. Malcolm kept on walking, as if nothing was wrong. When the unsuspecting teacher sat down, he jumped up suddenly with a yelp! Malcolm zipped out the door with a smile on his face.

Malcolm already had a record of misbehavior at the school, and this was the last straw. He was expelled. He didn't mind the expulsion, but he was taken aback to learn that he couldn't stay with the Gohannas, either. He was going to be sent to reform school.

Joe Louis (1914–1981)

In the 1930s, most big-time professional sports, such as baseball and basketball, were closed to African Americans. Boxing was the exception. In June 1937, the black boxer Joe Louis beat James J. Braddock, the white heavyweight champion, to become the first black heavyweight champion of the world. In June 1938, Louis defended his title against Max Schmeling, Adolf Hitler's champion of Germany.

Black people all over America celebrated Louis's victories. The Brown Bomber, as he was nicknamed, was a hero and a role model to many black boys who took up boxing as a sport.

A role model to many young African American boys, Joe Louis (left) is photographed boxing with Max Schmeling in 1936. Louis lost this match in the twelfth round, but beat Schmeling two years later. Louis held the world heavyweight title for more than eleven years.

CHAPTER 3

Malcolm the Mascot

I lived a thoroughly integrated life.

As it turned out, Malcolm was not sent directly to a reform school. Instead, in August 1939 he was sent first to a detention home—supposedly only until his case was heard by the juvenile court. The detention home in Mason, twelve miles from Lansing, wasn't a bad place at all. It was run by a nice white couple, Mrs. Lois Swerlein and her husband. They treated the boys in their care like family, even sitting down to eat with them.

Malcolm began to make himself useful around the detention home, sweeping and dusting. The Swerleins took a liking to him. They were friends with the judge in charge of Malcolm's case, and they arranged to have his hearings postponed over and over so that Malcolm could stay with them longer. They also arranged for him to attend Mason Junior High School.

Success in Junior High

Mason was an all-white town in 1939, except for one black family that had no children Malcolm's age. He was the only black student in his eighth grade class. Malcolm did well in school and became friendly with many of the white students. As he wryly remarked years later to the psychologist and author Kenneth Clark, "I lived a thoroughly integrated life."

A recent photo shows Maple Street in Mason, Michigan, where Malcolm tried his best to fit into the mostly white town.

During the school year of 1939–40, Malcolm joined the Mason Junior High basketball team, the band, and the debating club. He attended other school activities, including the dances. He understood, without anyone telling him, that it was all right for him to show up at a dance and look on from the sidelines. However, he was not supposed to dance with the white girls. At that time, white people strongly disapproved of African American boys dating white girls.

Just as in the elementary school in Lansing, students and teachers casually called Malcolm racist names like "nigger" and "coon." For the most part, they didn't mean to offend him, and for the most part, he wasn't even conscious of the insults. It was the 1930s, and most African Americans who suffered the barbs of racism did not allow themselves to think about fighting back when called these names, or even to think of the racial names as hateful. It was a fact of life that whites had the power to take their jobs away, to send them to prison, and sometimes to kill them. Black people, even black nationalists like Earl and Louise Little, taught their children by example not to confront white people. Malcolm did not realize until years afterward how deeply he had been **brainwashed** by his family, friends, schoolmates, teachers, neighbors, books, movies—the whole society he lived in.

Although Malcolm liked the subject of history, he disliked his history teacher, who continually made racial jokes. It was obvious the teacher enjoyed humiliating Malcolm. Once, when the class came to the "Negro history" section in the textbook, the teacher read it out loud, laughing. It was one paragraph long.

Malcolm's English teacher, on the other hand, seemed to genuinely care about him. Malcolm enjoyed English class, and he listened closely to the teacher's advice to the class on how to "become something in life." Malcolm was one of the best students in the eighth grade and for the most part had no behavior problems in this school.

Gone With the Wind

The movie *Gone With the Wind*, based on the Pulitzer Prize–winning novel by Margaret Mitchell, swept the Academy Awards in 1940. It was hailed as "the greatest movie ever made." Both the book and the movie, set in Georgia during the Civil War, presented the slave-owning South as a great civilization. In *Gone With the Wind*, the black characters were either contented slaves or (after Emancipation) miserable freedmen. The slave girl Prissy, played by the actress Butterfly McQueen, was an especially witless and silly black character.

This poster advertises the movie *Gone With the Wind*.

In fact, Malcolm became so popular at school that he was elected president of his class. Malcolm proudly reported his victory to Mr. and Mrs. Swerlein, who beamed with pride. It seemed that Malcolm was completely reformed, without even having to go to reform school.

Most of the time, Malcolm managed to ignore reminders that he lived in a racist society. For example, like everyone else in Mason, Malcolm went to see the movie *Gone With the Wind* when it was shown in the theaters. However, none of his white friends saw the movie the way he did. He was especially embarrassed by the character called Prissy, who was played by actress Butterfly McQueen. "I was the only Negro in the theater," he said. "When Butterfly McQueen went into her act, I felt like crawling under the rug."

Butterfly McQueen (right) as Prissy in the 1939 movie *Gone With the Wind.* Vivien Leigh (left) plays Scarlett O'Hara. Movies of that time routinely depicted black people as unintelligent and comical.

Malcolm's Boston Family

Around this time, Malcolm's half sister Ella came from Boston to visit. Malcolm had never met Ella or any of the children of Earl Little's first wife before, and he was surprised at the way Ella looked and acted. Like Malcolm's father, she was big and dark-skinned. She actually seemed *proud* of being black. Ella thought it was wrong that Malcolm and some of the other Little children had been placed in white foster homes.

Ella was deeply committed to helping family members, and she had already helped many relatives from Georgia settle in Boston. She immediately took a special interest in smart, likeable Malcolm. When Ella asked to see his report cards, Malcolm proudly showed off his good grades. She praised him for his election as class president.

Malcolm was strongly drawn to Ella with her motherly, take-charge ways. Malcolm was around fourteen years old when Ella invited him to visit her, and he made the long bus trip alone from Lansing to Boston. He had never been so far away from home, and it was like traveling to a different world.

Malcolm's Boston relatives lived in Roxbury, the black section of the city. They had a three-story house in a respectable neighborhood. Ella's mother, Daisy Mason, ran a profitable store. Ella owned a share in the business and worked alongside her mother.

During the early 1940s, Malcolm lived with his half sister Ella at her home on 72 Dale Street, in a section of Boston called Roxbury. The house is shown in this 1998 photo. An attempt is being made to preserve the house as a historic landmark.

In Boston, Malcolm was welcomed by Ella and her family: her younger sister, Mary; her third husband, Kenneth Collins; and Malcolm's aunt Sarah Alice ("Sas") and aunt Gracie, who were Earl Little's sisters. This branch of the Little family had weathered the hard times of the Great Depression fairly well, and they were able to stay together. For Malcolm, one of seven children in a poor family with a widowed mother, it was heavenly to be praised and fussed over by his newfound relatives.

Ella dreamed of having a lawyer in the family, and she felt sure that Malcolm was intelligent and self-assured enough to earn a law degree. She thought he just needed love and discipline from a strong family.

A New Outlook on Life

The Boston Little family was also connected with the wilder side of Roxbury. Malcolm's half brother, Earl Little, Jr., was a singer and dancer who wore flashy outfits and entertained at nightclubs. When Earl Jr. introduced Malcolm to the famous black singer Billie Holiday, Malcolm was thrilled.

In Roxbury, Malcolm found himself surrounded by crowds of black people. He had never in his life been with so many people like him. He was dazzled by the glamour of city life: fashionably dressed partygoers in nightclubs,

As a youth, Malcolm met the famous Billie Holiday, who is still considered one of the greatest jazz singers of all time. This portrait photo by Carl Van Vechten was taken in 1949.

bars, and dance halls where famous bands played. At the end of his visit, Malcolm returned to Michigan with a different outlook.

Back in Mason, Malcolm was no longer content. For the first time, it bothered him when Mr. and Mrs. Swerlein used racist language such as "nigger" in front of him. It also occurred to Malcolm that at school, he was more like a mascot than a real member of his class. Everyone liked him, but they didn't consider him one of them. He became more and more discontented. If someone made a racial slur, he would give that person a hard look. People began noticing his changed attitude. "You don't seem like yourself, Malcolm," Mrs. Swerlein said. "What's the matter?"

A Dream Destroyed

Toward the end of the semester, Malcolm had a memorable conversation with his favorite teacher. "Malcolm," the English teacher said one day when they were alone in the classroom, "you ought to be thinking about a career." Malcolm had just started to think about a career for himself, thanks to Ella and her ambitions for him. Since the teacher was always encouraging his students to look ahead and aim for success, and since Malcolm was one of the best students in the school, it seemed natural for him to take an interest in Malcolm's career. Malcolm blurted out, "I've been thinking I'd like to be a lawyer."

The English teacher looked very surprised. He answered Malcolm kindly, "You've got to be realistic about being a nigger. A lawyer—that's no realistic goal for a nigger." Malcolm might do very well as a carpenter, though, he suggested.

Malcolm was too shocked and hurt to argue. In the following weeks, he brooded about what his teacher had said. Was it "unrealistic" for him to try to become a lawyer? On the one hand, Malcolm didn't know any black lawyers. Some of the black people in Lansing had college degrees, but they were lucky to get a job as a janitor in a law firm or as a waiter at the Lansing Country Club. If a black college graduate was very lucky, he might be hired as a mailman.

On the other hand—why *couldn't* Malcolm become a lawyer? He was smarter than most of the boys and girls in his class, including the ones the English teacher encouraged to go to college. The question ate away at him. In class, he couldn't see any point in studying, if he was blocked from following his ambitions. With his white friends, he couldn't be easygoing, likeable Mascot Malcolm anymore.

He answered Malcolm kindly, "…A lawyer— that's no realistic goal for a nigger."

Finally Mrs. Swerlein and Malcolm's state social worker, Mr. Allyn, had a talk with him. It was obvious, they said reproachfully, that he was no longer happy at the detention home. So they arranged for him to live with the only black family in Mason, the Lyonses, who were friends of the Littles.

Malcolm managed to stay in school at Mason Junior High and finish the eighth grade. After graduation, though, he didn't know where he would live or what he would do. He wrote to Ella, asking if he could come live with her.

Ella wished she could take in all seven of her half brothers and sisters. She admired Wilfred and Hilda for keeping their household going, and her heart went out to poor Louise in the Kalamazoo State Mental Hospital. Ella wrote back to Malcolm that his Boston family missed him and thought about him all the time. If his mind was made up to live with them permanently, she would send him bus fare.

CHAPTER 4

Lured by the Nightlife

New York was heaven to me. And Harlem was Seventh Heaven!

Early in 1941, Malcolm arrived in Boston to live with his Little relatives. Ella, who never had an opportunity for a good education or a professional career, was eager to turn Malcolm into a lawyer. Aunt Sas and Aunt Gracie were eager to turn Malcolm into a good Baptist and a gentleman.

Ella and the aunts lived on the Hill, the upper-middle-class section of Roxbury. The black people on the Hill considered themselves better than the black people in the bars and pool halls on Massachusetts Avenue. They were careful to talk and behave in a "cultured" and "cultivated" way and to dress conservatively, like the white Bostonians they admired. Ella's plan was to fit Malcolm into that way of life.

Ella found Malcolm a respectable part-time job at Walker's Auto Parks Company, a parking lot business owned by her uncle, John Walker. She took Malcolm to church on Sundays, and she was happy when he sang in the church choir. She urged him to get to know the "nice young people" his age on the Hill. But Malcolm was an adventurous, curious fifteen-year-old boy from the Midwest, who was eager to experience more of the sophisticated city life.

Becoming a Cool Cat

Malcolm was drawn to the world of pool halls, nightclubs, and dance halls in the ghetto section of Roxbury. He admired the "cool cats" with long, straight, "conked" hairstyles and loud-colored zoot suits.

To Ella's dismay, Malcolm made friends with Malcolm Jarvis, or Shorty, a young man who worked at a pool hall. Shorty taught Malcolm the street lingo of Roxbury, and he helped Malcolm "conk" his hair.

In the 1940s, black Americans who wanted to look fashionable would straighten their tightly curled hair with a harsh chemical mixture called congolene. Barbershops would do "conks," but Shorty showed Malcolm how they could save money by doing their own.

Shorty mixed sliced potatoes in a jar with lye, and then stirred in two eggs. After he rubbed Malcolm's head with Vaseline, he combed the lye mixture through his hair. Malcolm felt as if his head was on fire. But after Shorty washed out the lye, Malcolm was pleased with his newly straight, "white" hair. He continued getting "conks" for the next several years.

One time, while visiting his brother in Michigan, after Malcolm

These teenage boys in zoot suits were photographed in 1943. Malcolm proudly sent a picture of himself in his first zoot suit to his brothers and sisters in Lansing.

had covered his scalp with the lye mixture, he discovered that all the pipes in the house were frozen. The only water in the house was in the toilet bowl—so he stuck his head in it to wash off the mixture. Later in life, when he looked back in disgust over this period, Malcolm thought this incident showed exactly how low he had sunk.

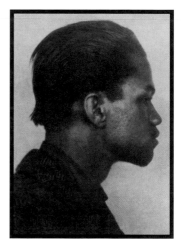

This 1944 Boston police mug shot of Malcolm shows his conked hairstyle. Arrested for stealing his aunt Gracie's fur coat, he was given a three-month suspended sentence.

Malcolm's half brother, Earl Jr., was happy to introduce him to Roxbury's nightlife. He helped Malcolm sneak out of the house and took him to the bars and nightclubs where he entertained. Malcolm looked so much older than his real age that he was allowed in.

Ella's husband, Kenneth, also liked to dress "cool" and spend time in the ghetto. He worked as a shoeshine boy at the Roseland State Ballroom. When he decided to quit, he taught Malcolm to take over his job—to Ella's disapproval.

Hustling

Shining shoes at a dance hall wasn't the kind of respectable job that Ella had in mind for fifteen-year-old Malcolm. Malcolm, on the other hand, couldn't imagine a better place to work than at the Roseland. All the famous swing bands played there, led by people like Duke Ellington, Count Basie, and Artie Shaw. White people as well as black flocked to the Roseland, where there were separate evenings for white and "colored" people.

Earl Jr. died of tuberculosis in the fall of 1941, but Kenneth Collins and Shorty continued to introduce Malcolm to the fast life in Roxbury. They took him to parties where he smoked, drank liquor, and used illegal drugs, such as marijuana. He learned to do the Lindy Hop, the lively swing dance that was all the rage. He also bought a zoot suit on credit.

Working at the shoeshine parlor in the Roseland Ballroom, Malcolm was soon making good tips by shining shoes with flair and handing out towels in the men's washroom. Malcolm also quickly learned how to "hustle," or to get ahead by tricky or illegal means. He began to sell marijuana to his shoeshine customers and learned how to spot and avoid policemen in plain clothes.

Ella strongly disapproved of Malcolm's undisciplined ways, because she knew he was hurting his chances for success. She was often angry with him, and she lectured him every time she got a chance. Still, she wasn't about to give up on her lovable, smart brother.

Many Jobs

For his part, Malcolm was grateful to Ella and didn't want to disappoint her. He accepted the "respectable" full-time job she got him in place of his shoe-shining job. He was a "soda jerk," serving ice cream sundaes and sodas at the

Duke Ellington, composer, orchestra leader, and pianist, is shown in this 1943 photo. Ellington was one of the most influential musicians in jazz and generally in American music.

Townsend Drug and Soda Fountain, near Ella's house. Ella considered this job a good way to meet "nice young people."

Malcolm was not happy with this work. For one thing, he disliked being called a soda jerk. The young people of the neighborhood he did meet seemed *too* young to Malcolm. Every evening after work, he would sneak out of the house to dance and party until early in the morning. He lived a double life—his respectable life and his ghetto life. Fortunately, he didn't need much sleep.

By the winter of 1941, Malcolm had a job as a bus boy at the Parker House Hotel. On December 7, the Japanese bombed the U.S. military base at Pearl Harbor in Hawaii, and the United States entered World War II.

U.S. battleships at Pearl Harbor, Hawaii, photographed during the Japanese bombing on December 7, 1941. The attack aroused patriotic fervor in thousands of Americans but not in Malcolm.

Ella wished Malcolm could have joined the army, to get him away from the bad influences in Roxbury. However, he was too young, only sixteen and a half at the time of Pearl Harbor. The minimum age for military service was eighteen. This suited Malcolm fine, because he didn't want to join the army, anyway. He and many other young black men from poor backgrounds felt no obligation to fight for a country in which they were second-class citizens. As Shorty said, "Whitey owns everything. He wants us to go and bleed for him? Let him fight."

Fortunately the war opened up other job opportunities. The railroads needed men to replace porters and other workers who had been drafted, or required to serve in the army. Ella thought working on the railroad, like the army, would be good for Malcolm by removing him from Roxbury. Again through Ella's connections, Malcolm got a job with the New Haven Railroad. He worked as a dishwasher and then a sandwich boy on the Yankee Clipper, a train that made the Boston–New York City run.

Heavenly Harlem

During layovers in New York City, Malcolm fell in love with Harlem—the black section of Manhattan. To him, Harlem made Roxbury look unsophisticated. It was the home of sophisticated black people—of stars such as the singers Ella Fitzgerald, Dinah Washington, and Billie Holiday. Harlem, Malcolm felt, was where he truly belonged. As he stated years later in his autobiography, "New York was heaven to me. And Harlem was Seventh Heaven!"

Between the trips to and from Boston, Malcolm spent all his spare time in Harlem. One of his favorite haunts was Small's Paradise, a bar and restaurant on Seventh Avenue. Malcolm was impressed with the lowlife customers at Small's: con men, pimps, prostitutes, and gamblers. He also loved hanging around the

A woman entertains customers at Small's Paradise Club in a photo from 1929. In the 1940s, Malcolm hung out at Small's and worked there as a waiter.

Braddock Hotel, where some of the best black musicians performed. He made friends with many well-known entertainers.

Even though Malcolm enjoyed his new life, he became restless. In October 1942, Malcolm quit his railroad job and went back to Lansing to see his brothers and sisters. With his stylish clothes and his hip New York slang, he impressed the people who used to know him. Sadly, when Malcolm visited his mother at Kalamazoo State Mental Hospital, she hardly recognized him.

Malcolm remained in Michigan for several months. He worked at a variety of jobs, legal and illegal, never staying with anything very long. He worked for a jewelry store in Lansing and for a sparkplug company in Flint. By March 1943, he was back in New York, working for the railroad.

Before long Malcolm's high life in New York spilled over into his railroad job, and he began to show up at work half drunk. He was rude to passengers, and after several complaints, the New Haven Railroad fired him.

Malcolm didn't care, because World War II was in progress, and jobs were plentiful. There was a steady stream of soldiers and sailors on leave, passing through New York—with money to spend. Malcolm got a job working as a waiter at Small's Paradise.

Harlem

Black people have lived in New York City since 1683, when it was a Dutch settlement called New Amsterdam. During the course of New York's history, black people have populated various parts of the city. Early in the twentieth century, Harlem, which is located in the northern section of Manhattan Island, became the center of the African American community in New York.

During the 1920s, when Marcus Garvey was promoting black pride, culture blossomed in Harlem. In literature, the poet Langston Hughes and the novelist Zora Neale Hurston made their mark. Harlem's famous Cotton Club promoted many performers who became world-renowned, such as bandleaders Duke Ellington and Count Basie, and singers Lena Horne and Billie Holiday.

Harlem, 125th Street and Lenox Avenue, photographed in 1950. In the late 1980s, Lenox Avenue was renamed Malcolm X Boulevard, and this part of 125th Street has been renamed Martin Luther King, Jr. Boulevard.

Draft-dodging

Malcolm's younger brother Reginald was a merchant mariner, working on the commercial ships that delivered troops and supplies for the armed forces. He visited Malcolm when he was on leave. Malcolm enjoyed his brother's company, talking over the old days in Lansing and impressing Reginald with his big-city sophistication.

This photo shows an enlistment office in Queens, New York, in 1941. For the first time, the Army Air Corps allowed African American men to enlist, and unlike Malcolm, many of them chose to serve.

When Malcolm turned eighteen in 1943, the U.S. draft board ordered him to register for military service. Malcolm showed up for his induction examination, but he had no intention of being drafted. He'd heard of ways to fool the draft board into rejecting him.

Malcolm chose to act crazy—dangerously crazy, so much so, that he was able to convince an army psychiatrist to find him mentally unfit for service. Malcom was issued a 4-F card, relieving him of his service obligations.

To Malcolm, dodging the draft was a joke, a prank. He didn't see that he actually was on a road to destruction.

CHAPTER 5

From Paradise to Hell

I had sunk to the very bottom of the American white man's society.

Between 1942 and 1946, Malcolm kept on the move, dividing his time between Boston and Harlem.

When Malcolm was in Boston, he stayed with Ella. She was outraged by many things he did, and she constantly kept after him to straighten out his life. She was especially horrified that he had a white girlfriend whose name was Sophia. Ella saw this relationship as an insult to his race, but Malcolm thought it gave him higher status. Ella also knew that dating a white woman was dangerous. Nothing upset racist whites more than an interracial couple. Many black men had been killed just for *looking* at a white woman.

A Life of Crime

Eventually Malcolm lost his job at Small's Paradise in Harlem. He was sorry, because he enjoyed the social life at Small's. His friend Sammy helped him get started selling illegal drugs in Harlem. Soon Malcolm was making a good income from those drug sales. He couldn't see that this way of living would lead to a dead end.

Before long, Malcolm became known to the Harlem police as a drug dealer, and they began watching him closely. When selling drugs became difficult, Malcolm began committing robberies. He also started carrying a

MALCOLM

—Right Thumb

—Left Thumb

Four fingers

and

pistol. To give himself courage before a holdup, he used cocaine, a hard drug, and eventually became addicted to it. As his cocaine habit became more expensive to maintain, he stole more often.

Malcolm took bigger and bigger risks during his burglary jobs, until finally his partner, Sammy, was wounded during a getaway. Sammy and Malcolm had a violent quarrel, and Malcolm decided to drop the burglary business.

Next Malcolm began working in the "numbers" business—an extremely popular but illegal type of gambling lottery. He was a "numbers runner," delivering his customers' betting slips to the numbers bankers.

Almost everyone in Harlem played the numbers, hoping for a big payoff, just as people today buy state lottery tickets—only lottery tickets are legal. Malcolm could see that the people getting rich from the numbers were the bankers, not the players. Still, he always placed bets himself.

Malcolm placed his own bets with West Indian Archie, a numbers man with a gift for remembering numbers. He never had to write a customer's number down, and so he never risked

This photo shows police officers arresting a black looter from a storefront during a riot in Harlem, August 1943. After the riot, many white customers stopped going to Harlem nightclubs and dance halls.

getting caught with proof of his illegal dealings. Malcolm admired West Indian Archie and other clever numbers men. "If they had lived in another kind of society," he mused later, "their exceptional mathematical talents might have been better used. But they were black."

As for Malcolm's own talents, he used them to make money any way he could. He even sought out customers for prostitutes and transported illegal liquor.

In 1945, Malcolm and West Indian Archie quarreled over a bet Malcolm had placed. Archie said Malcolm's numbers hadn't won. Malcolm said that Archie's famous memory was failing him. West Indian Archie, to protect his reputation, threatened to kill Malcolm.

Get Malcolm

Other people wanted to kill Malcolm, too. A man who looked something like him had robbed a bar at gunpoint, and the owners blamed Malcolm. In another bar, Malcolm punched a young crook, who vowed to get even—with a knife.

Some policemen advised Malcolm to get out of town if he wanted to keep on living. By now, Malcolm was having trouble thinking straight. His only thoughts were about staying high on drugs. He took everything he could get his hands on: opium, amphetamines, marijuana.

Some policemen advised Malcolm to get out of town, if he wanted to keep on living.

Malcolm would almost certainly have been killed, one way or another, if he had stayed in New York. But miraculously, Sammy— Malcolm's ex-partner in burglary—called Malcolm's friend Shorty in Boston and asked him to take Malcolm home before it was too late. Shorty drove from Boston to Harlem, found Malcolm wandering the streets, and took him back to Roxbury.

Although Ella was deeply disappointed in Malcolm, she still tried to help him. She got his old job back for him at the Walker Auto Park in downtown Boston. Malcolm, however, continued his drug habit. He needed more and more money to pay for it, so he started a burglary ring that included Shorty, a friend of Shorty's, and Shorty and Malcolm's white girlfriends.

The young women would get into wealthy homes in white neighborhoods by pretending to be saleswomen or students taking a poll. Then they would let Malcolm know where the valuables were located in a house, as well as when the owners would be away. Later the three men would perform the actual robbery, and Malcolm would sell the stolen goods.

Arrested

Malcolm's gang pulled off several burglaries without getting caught, but the Boston police suspected Malcolm. Finally, when he took a stolen watch in for repair, they arrested him. Malcolm was tried for armed robbery and sentenced to eight to ten years in prison.

Ella and Malcolm's younger brother Reginald were in the courtroom when Malcolm was sentenced. Ella was indignant that Malcolm received the maximum sentence, while the two white women in his burglary ring got off with only a few months probation. To Malcolm's family it seemed like typical racial injustice.

Ella was also angry with Malcolm for getting himself into such serious trouble. If Malcolm had listened to her, he could have had a law degree by now. Instead of going to prison, he could have been fighting the injustices suffered by his people.

As a convict entering Charlestown State Prison, Malcolm was thoroughly fingerprinted.

In February 1946, Malcolm was sent to Charlestown State Prison, near Boston. The prison was more than a hundred years old and infested with rats and lice. The cells, barely big enough for one cot, had no running water. For a toilet, each cell had a bucket.

Caged

The worst thing about prison for Malcolm—worse than the stink of the toilet buckets—were the steel bars. He was in a cage. He never forgot how that felt.

Soon after Malcolm started serving his prison sentence, Ella went to visit him. She was angry to find that he wasn't sorry for all the worry and trouble he'd caused his family. In fact, he wasn't sorry about anything except getting caught. Furthermore, he was still using drugs, bought from the prison guards. Ella had thought that some prison time might persuade Malcolm to go straight, but now she wondered.

For several months Malcolm was in a nasty mood, making life difficult for himself and for everyone around him. He swore at the prison psychologist and the prison chaplain. He talked back to the guards, smoked in nonsmoking areas, and broke any number of other prison rules.

Still, Malcolm's family didn't give up on him. Aunt Sas and Aunt Gracie were sure that religion could save him. They kept urging him, during visits and in their letters, to accept Christianity. He told Ella not to bring them to visit anymore. To anyone who would listen, he said all the insulting things he could think of about the Bible and God. The other prisoners nicknamed him "Satan."

Use Your Brains

Then Malcolm started paying attention to another prisoner, one he called Bimbi. Malcolm noticed that both the guards and the other prisoners respected Bimbi, even though he didn't talk tough—the way Malcolm did. Bimbi talked about what he *knew*—history, theology, literature. When he talked, everyone listened. Malcolm was impressed.

The two men became friends, and Bimbi advised Malcolm to use his brains. He meant that Malcolm should read the books in the prison library and take correspondence courses to educate himself. Malcolm read all kinds of books—Shakespearean plays, the Bible, Aesop's fables, and classic novels such as *Moby Dick*—and then discussed them with Bimbi. Suddenly, Malcolm seemed to be picking up where he had left off at school—when he was one of the best students at Mason Junior High.

CHAPTER 6

Discovering the Nation of Islam

You don't even know who you are.
—*Malcolm's brother Reginald*

Malcolm was using his brains now, but he wasn't reformed. He still used drugs and gambled. He ran a booking operation for prisoners who wanted to bet on sports events. At the beginning of 1947, Malcolm was sent from Charlestown to Concord Reformatory. Wilfred, Hilda, Philbert, and Reginald sent Malcolm many letters and went to visit when they could. They discussed with each other and with Ella how to get their brother out of prison and to make sure he never went there again.

Ella visited him, bringing along her baby son, Rodnell. As Rodnell grew older, he loved to sit on his uncle's knee and listen to stories. Malcolm worked in the prison furniture shop, and in his spare time, he made a little table and chair for his nephew.

One of Malcolm's few pleasures in prison was listening to boxing matches and ball games on the radio. He followed African American baseball player Jackie Robinson's career with extra zeal. A few months after Malcolm arrived in Concord, Robinson made history by being the first African American to play major league baseball.

Jackie Robinson (1919–1972)

Born in Cairo, Georgia, Jackie Robinson broke the "color" line of baseball and joined the Brooklyn Dodgers in April 1947. He was a second baseman for them and had a batting average of .311 and a talent for stealing bases. Fans joked that the only thing he ever stole were bases. Before joining the Dodgers, he had played in the Negro American League. After joining the Dodgers, he was named Rookie of the Year that first year and held the National League's Most Valuable Player honor in 1949.

Jackie Robinson was a hero to many black Americans, including Malcolm. "When he played," said Malcolm, "my ear was glued to the radio." In 1962, Robinson was elected to the Baseball Hall of Fame.

Jackie Robinson is photographed in his Dodgers uniform in 1947. The first African American to join a major league team, Robinson had to endure racial insults from both players and fans, as well as prove his athletic ability.

A New Religion

While Malcolm was at Concord, he began to hear about the religion of Islam. In Detroit, his older brother Wilfred had just joined the Nation of Islam (NOI), and he was sure that this religion was the answer for the rest of the family, too. Soon Hilda, Philbert, Reginald, and Wesley also joined the Nation.

This photo from 1963 shows Malcolm X (center) with his brothers Wilfred X (left) and Philbert X (right). From Malcolm's conversion to the NOI until 1964, the brothers were all followers of Elijah Muhammad.

Although Philbert had always been the one in the family who was most enthusiastic about Christianity, he now wrote Malcolm an excited letter about the Nation of Islam. He advised Malcolm to "pray to Allah (God) for deliverance." Malcolm had never taken Philbert's advice about anything, and he still thought all religions were nonsense. He wrote Philbert a rude reply.

Then Reginald sent Malcolm a seemingly casual, friendly letter. He ended the letter, "Malcolm, don't eat any more pork, and don't smoke any more cigarettes. I'll show you how to get out of prison."

How to get out of prison! That caught Malcolm's attention. He thought his brother must have known some trick to make the prison authorities let him out. He had no idea that Reginald was talking about Islam.

Malcolm did stop eating pork and smoking, and he was surprised how good that made him feel about himself. His mother, he remembered, had always refused to eat pork. Now Malcolm was proving that he was able to discipline himself, and it did wonders for his self-esteem. The other prisoners seemed to respect him more, too.

Norfolk Prison Colony

In 1948, Ella managed to get Malcolm transferred from the Concord prison to Norfolk Prison Colony. The philosophy of this facility was not just to punish prisoners but to help prisoners turn their lives around. Then when they were released, they could be useful members of society.

There were walls around Norfolk, but no bars on the rooms, and each prisoner had his own room. There was a fine library that prisoners could use. There were also courses for them to take, as well as a debate program to develop their thinking and speaking skills.

All this time Malcolm never understood how Reginald was going to get him out of prison. Finally Reginald visited Malcolm and told him that the real prison was his brainwashed mind. For centuries, Reginald explained, black people had been enslaved and deceived by white people. Now, thanks to the Nation of Islam, African Americans were beginning to discover their proud history. The white man's time of domination was almost over, and the Nation of Islam was leading black people to their destiny.

Malcolm was stunned by Reginald's message. As he listened carefully to the startling ideas of the Nation of Islam, everything about Malcolm's life began to fall into place for him. Malcolm focused on the phrase "The white man is the devil," which rationally was a ridiculous idea. Yet,

Malcolm was stunned by Reginald's message.

Nation of Islam

The Nation of Islam was founded in about 1930 in Detroit by Wallace D. Fard, a silk peddler. His followers believed that he had come from Mecca, the Muslim holy city in Saudi Arabia. In 1936, Fard disappeared, and Elijah Muhammad, one of Fard's assistants, became the leader of the NOI. Muhammad was called "The Messenger" because his followers believed that Fard represented Allah in human form and that Muhammad had received the truth directly from Fard.

In some ways, Black Muslims (the popular name for Nation of Islam) carried on Marcus Garvey's ideas. They taught that blacks were naturally superior to whites. Furthermore, they taught that all white people were enemies of black people. The natural religion for African Americans, they believed, was not Christianity, but Islam.

Members of the Nation of Islam were expected to live disciplined lives, giving up tobacco, alcohol, and "unclean" foods, such as pork. They must treat each other like family but avoid white people as much as possible. Just as Garvey had recommended, they were to create their own stores and other businesses to become economically independent of whites. Eventually, they intended to establish a separate all-black nation.

when Malcolm thought about the white people he had known, he felt all of them had had some ill effect on him: the social workers in Lansing, his teachers at Mason Junior High, and the judge who sent Malcolm and Shorty to prison for ten years—to name just a few. Malcolm realized that none of these white people had had his interests at heart—even when they thought they were helping him.

A young black man, photographed in 1992, wears a Malcolm X T-shirt and an "X" baseball cap. For some African Americans, "The white man is the devil" still resonates.

To Malcolm and many other African Americans who had suffered from racism, "The white man is the devil" felt exactly right in their deepest souls.

A Message from Allah

"You don't even know who you are," Reginald told him. What was his real family name? Not "Little"—that was obviously a former white master's name. What was his *African* name? Lost. What was his family's African language? Lost.

Black people, Malcolm realized, could never gain self-respect by trying to become white. That was true for the "respectable" black people on the Hill in Roxbury, who tried so hard to act and talk like Boston upper-class people. It was just as true for Malcolm and the other "cool cats" in the bars and nightclubs, so proud of their long, straight, white-looking conked hair, so eager to attract a white girlfriend.

African Americans could never lift themselves up by selling out other black folk. Malcolm was ashamed as he remembered all the times he had robbed, cheated, or threatened other black people, including his friends.

The key, Reginald told Malcolm, lay in the true religion of the black race, which was not European Christianity—according to Reginald and the Nation of Islam. Christianity was a white man's religion, which taught blacks to submit humbly to mistreatment. No, their true religion was the one they had lost when their African ancestors were enslaved and uprooted from their culture.

Their religion, Reginald explained, was now rediscovered, thanks to a man named Elijah Muhammad. He brought black Americans a message from Allah. He taught that the original religion of the black race was Islam. By practicing Islam, African Americans could gain self-respect and love and help each other. That was the mission of the Nation of Islam.

In this photo from the 1950s, Elijah Muhammad greets a new convert to the Nation of Islam. He had a kind, fatherly manner with his followers.

CHAPTER 7

Education Behind Bars

I knew right there in prison that reading had changed forever the course of my life.

Now Malcolm read with a burning purpose. He read to find information to back up Elijah Muhammad's teachings. He devoured everything he could find about black history and culture in America and the rest of the world. For the first time, he learned that black people had developed great civilizations in Africa long ago. During the Middle Ages in Europe, educated people knew that one of the finest universities in the world was in Timbuktu, Mali, in western Africa.

History of Blacks in America

Malcolm also learned the history of slavery in America. From the early seventeenth century until the Civil War, more than a million Africans had been torn from their communities, enslaved, and shipped across the Atlantic Ocean under horrific conditions. They spent their lives as unpaid workers for white slave owners. Many American whites had grown rich in the slave trade, and many American whites—including heroes like George Washington and Thomas Jefferson—had owned estates worked by slaves. Congress outlawed the importation of slaves in 1808, but the slave trade continued illegally right up to the Civil War.

This idealized 1851 painting shows George Washington (in the black suit) on his country estate with his black slaves, who are unrealistically depicted as having an easy farm life.

Black slaves had not just been victims, Malcolm learned. They had been leaders and fighters, too. He read about the black soldiers, thousands of them, who had fought in the American Revolution. He also found out about the slave uprisings led by Nat Turner in Virginia and Toussaint Louverture in Haiti. It made him all the angrier to remember his history teacher at Mason Junior High, reading the one paragraph in the textbook about "Negro history," and laughing. The American education system had obviously been teaching a "whitened" version of American history.

"True Knowledge" of the Black Race

Reginald reported to his brothers and sisters in Michigan that Malcolm seemed very interested in the Nation of Islam. They followed up Reginald's visit with a steady stream of letters, encouraging Malcolm to join the group. The brothers and sisters scraped up the money for Hilda to travel from Detroit to Massachusetts to visit him.

In long, earnest conversations, Hilda explained what Elijah Muhammad taught about the races. She told Malcolm that according to Muhammad, Allah was

She told Malcolm that according to Elijah Muhammad, Allah was black, and the original human beings were black.

"Whitened" History

Until fairly recently, the history of African Americans, and all they had accomplished in spite of being oppressed, had been absent from textbooks, movies, and other media. All that most students, black or white, learned was that African Americans

were slaves until the Civil War, and that President Lincoln freed them with the Emancipation Proclamation.

There was no mention that black soldiers fought bravely in the American Revolution, the Civil War, and World Wars I and II. The many contributions that blacks made to American life—including science, music, dance, and literature—were mostly ignored.

These two African American Civil War soldiers were photographed in uniform, c. 1860–1870. Before increased awareness of the contributions made by African Americans, it was scarcely known that about 180,000 blacks, or about ten percent of the Union army and navy, fought in the Civil War.

black, and the original humans were black. Whites were an inferior race, created six thousand years ago by an evil scientist named Yakub. Through lies, murder, and other evil acts, the white race had conquered and ruled the black race. Now, Muhammad taught, the whites' time of domination was up. Soon Allah would destroy them all.

Malcolm listened to everything Hilda told him. He was stunned speechless. It was a bizarre, incredible story—and yet at its core, Malcolm believed, were powerful ideas: On the one hand, white people were to blame for the present dismal condition of blacks—for brutalizing them and keeping them poor and ignorant. On the other hand, black people couldn't expect whites to help them. It was foolish for blacks to try to merge with whites. The only solution was for blacks to become self-sufficient and independent.

Hilda's visit made such an impression on Malcolm that he wrote to Elijah Muhammad himself. Malcolm was deeply moved when the leader of the Nation of Islam replied in a personal letter. Muhammad welcomed Malcolm into the "true knowledge" and even enclosed a small amount of money for Malcolm's necessities in prison.

Malcolm was almost ready to join the Nation of Islam, but he faced a serious stumbling block: He would have to begin praying regularly. Daily prayer, facing east toward the holy city of Mecca, kneeling and bowing, was required of all faithful Muslims.

All over the world, Muslims pray daily facing Mecca, as in this photograph taken in a mosque.

This was a big hurdle for Malcolm's pride. All these years, he'd thought he didn't have to kneel to anyone, even God. It took him a week before he could finally admit that he needed forgiveness, and forced himself down on his knees to pray. Gradually, during the course of 1948, he completely converted to his new religion.

Now Malcolm wrote to Elijah Muhammad daily, as well as to his own brothers and sisters. Wanting to express himself better, he took a course in penmanship. He requested a dictionary and studied it from front to back, copying the words and definitions, one page at a time. As Malcolm learned the words, he also found himself learning bits of history, science, and much more.

Freedom Through Books

At the same time, Malcolm found the world of books opening up to him. The more he learned, the more he understood what he read. The more he understood what he read, the more the books transported him out of himself. When Malcolm was gripped by a book, he forgot that he was in prison.

He began to feel like a different person—the real Malcolm. As he put it later, "I knew right there in prison that reading had changed forever the course of my life." One author who made a deep impression on him was W.E.B. Du Bois, a black historian and early **civil rights** leader. "What, after all, am I?" wrote Du Bois. "Am I an American or am I a Negro? Can I be both?"

Malcolm hated to stop reading for anything—not even the lights-out at ten o'clock every night. There was a dim light in

This 1904 photo shows W.E.B. Du Bois, co-founder of the NAACP but later a critic of its emphasis on integration. In the last few years of his life, he moved to Ghana, where he died in 1963.

the hall outside his room—barely enough to read by if he sat on the floor by the door. There Malcolm would keep on reading late into the night. He strained his eyes so much that he began wearing glasses for the first time in his life.

Reginald and Ella continued to visit and encourage Malcolm. Ella wasn't sure about some of the Nation of Islam's teachings, and she hadn't joined yet. She could see, though, how Malcolm's new faith was transforming him. Ella was delighted that Malcolm wanted to educate himself.

Ella still hoped that Malcolm might become a lawyer. Because the prison authorities tried to keep law books away from the prisoners, she smuggled some in to him. On a visit, she would bring along her little son, Rodnell, with a book hidden in his pants.

Once Malcolm decided to join the Nation of Islam, he began looking for opportunities to educate other African Americans. He wrote dozens of letters to his friends outside the prison, but none of them paid any attention. He had better luck with his fellow prisoners, especially after he joined the debating program for prisoners at Norfolk.

A Talent for Public Speaking

Malcolm prepared intensively for each weekly debate. Asking himself what his opponent's logical argument would be, he came up with arguments against it. Wherever possible, he slipped in some information about African American history, especially about how people of color had long been oppressed and abused by white people.

In the debating program, Malcolm discovered that he loved speaking to an audience, and he had a gift for it. Malcolm was good at thinking quickly in response to any debate point. He had

The FBI and Black Nationalism

Under J. Edgar Hoover, the Federal Bureau of Investigation (FBI) had been concerned about black nationalism. The bureau thought black nationalism was connected with revolutionary movements in Russia (the Union of Soviet Socialist Republics) and other countries, and it was afraid that black nationalists would work to overthrow the U.S. government.

J. Edgar Hoover, photographed in 1924, at the beginning of his 49-year-long career as director of the FBI. Hoover was suspicious of any group that criticized the U.S. government, including the Nation of Islam.

In the 1920s, the FBI followed Marcus Garvey and the UNIA closely, and in 1927, the bureau forced Garvey to leave the United States. Later, the FBI also monitored the Nation of Islam, and kept a file on Elijah Muhammad. Malcolm's letters from prison to Muhammad were opened and read. When he joined the Nation of Islam in 1948, the bureau began to follow Malcolm's activities and contacts as well.

facts at his fingertips to back up his arguments from all of the reading he had done.

In 1950, Malcolm was transferred from the Norfolk Prison Colony back to Charlestown. The Norfolk Prison authorities said Malcolm was being transferred because he had refused to have an inoculation for typhoid. Malcolm felt he was being punished for his success in persuading black convicts to join the Nation of Islam, which was under the watchful eye of the Federal Bureau of Investigation (FBI).

It was harder for Malcolm to find opportunities to speak to his fellow prisoners in the strict atmosphere of the Charlestown Prison, but he made his own chances. Working in the prison laundry, he preached to black convicts as they picked up their clean clothes. He joined a Bible class, as that was a popular activity with black prisoners.

In Bible class, Malcolm argued that Jesus couldn't have been blue-eyed and blond, the way whites often pictured him. In fact, Malcolm suggested, Jesus might have been black. The white teacher was upset, but grudgingly admitted that Jesus was probably "brown." The black students were electrified—and ready to hear more of Malcolm's ideas.

In 1951, Malcolm applied for parole, or early release from jail, but he was denied. Malcolm and his family thought the parole board had turned him down because of his work for the Nation of Islam. In the summer of 1952, Malcolm applied again, and this time he was finally granted parole. He had been in prison for six and a half years.

Malcolm proposed the notion that Jesus was black. This painting on a storefront in Los Angeles, California, in 1992 states that Jesus is a black man, and that the storeowner is also black.

CHAPTER 8

Black and Proud

*We didn't land on Plymouth Rock, my brothers and
sisters—Plymouth Rock landed on us!*

Malcolm's brother Wilfred was his parole sponsor,
guaranteeing that Malcolm had a place to live and
a job. Therefore, Malcolm had to move to Michigan. His
family all felt that he would be better off away from
Boston, and Malcolm had to agree. He had too many
connections there from his former criminal life. As soon
as Malcolm was released in August 1952, he took a bus
to Detroit.

A Fresh Start

In Detroit, Malcolm began his new life with Wilfred
and his family. He worked in the furniture store where
Wilfred was the manager. He joined the Detroit Nation of
Islam (NOI) temple, called Temple One because it was the
first NOI temple to be founded. Wilfred, Hilda, Philbert,
and Wesley were all active members there.

The Littles had done a great deal to revitalize the Nation
of Islam. Because their family life had been shattered when
they were young, it was especially satisfying for the Littles
to rejoin each other in this black nationalist group.
Together they were carrying on the values that Earl and
Louise Little had struggled for: black pride and black
independence.

The Littles were sad, however, that their brother Reginald was no longer in the Nation of Islam. Reginald had broken the NOI's rules against adultery, and Elijah Muhammad had suspended him. That meant that all members of the Nation of Islam, even his own brothers and sisters, were supposed to avoid him.

Malcolm found it especially hard to shun his brother, because Reginald was the one who had first led him to the Nation of Islam. However, he accepted Muhammad's decision. He refused to listen to Reginald's criticisms of Muhammad.

A New Way of Life

Living with Wilfred and his family, Malcolm was impressed with their orderly habits. Nothing could have been further from the chaotic life Malcolm had lived on the streets. Malcolm followed the family's daily morning routine of rising, washing, prayers, and breakfasting on juice and coffee. At work or school, all of them prayed again at noon and at three o'clock. They knew other Muslims all over the world were doing the same.

In Wilfred's house, there was none of the confusion and wrangling that Malcolm remembered from his childhood. Everyone in the family, even the children, greeted each other in quiet voices: "As-Salaam-Alaikum" (Peace be unto you), and the response, "Wa-Alaikum Salaam" (And unto you be peace). The Nation of Islam used Arabic phrases, because Arabic was the common language of Islam.

The temple was not only a place to worship on Sundays; it was also the central focus of the members' lives. They gathered at the temple on Wednesdays and Fridays for lectures on history, economics, and hygiene. Malcolm marveled to see the women dressed in long skirts and headscarves, the children neat and polite, the men in conservative suits. Malcolm was one of these quietly dressed men—his "conk" long since cut off for short, natural hair. He too greeted his fellow Muslims respectfully as "brother" and "sister."

When Malcolm joined the Nation of Islam in Detroit, it was only a small group. They could barely afford the storefront building they met in, which was located in a neighborhood near pig-slaughtering pens. This was especially disgusting for Muslims because of their belief that pigs and pork were unclean.

Outside the temple, the streets were full of black men and women ruining their health with drug and alcohol addiction, wasting their talents on hustling. Malcolm yearned to see all the African Americans in Detroit at Temple Number One. The other members of the temple seemed content to wait for Allah to send new recruits, but Malcolm itched to educate them, the way he had done in prison.

Meeting Elijah Muhammad

Only a few weeks after arriving in Detroit, Malcolm had the chance to see Elijah Muhammad, the man he considered his

At the NOI Savior's Day Convention in Chicago, Illinois, February 26, 1966, members attending are dressed in conservative, dignified clothes. Savior's Day celebrates the birthday of Wallace D. Fard, founder of the NOI.

This 1966 photo shows Elijah Muhammad (at podium) speaking to a Nation of Islam convention in Chicago, Illinois.

personal savior. All the Temple One members traveled in a car caravan from Detroit to Chicago, where Muhammad was based. Together with the members of Chicago's Temple Two, they formed an audience of about two hundred.

Malcolm was overcome with emotion when Muhammad walked into the hall. He was a slight, brown man with a sensitive face. Muhammad and the strapping bodyguards around him all wore dark suits, white shirts, and bow ties. Muhammad also wore a gold-embroidered fez, a type of cap with a tassel.

Malcolm drank in every word as Elijah Muhammad spoke. He was moved to hear the leader tell of the years he had spent in prison for defying the government. Malcolm nodded as Muhammad spoke of the blacks' centuries of bondage in "the wilderness of North America," brainwashed by the "blue-eyed devil white man" until they were "mentally, morally, and spiritually dead." Malcom felt empowered when he heard Muhammad explain that the knowledge of black culture and history would raise black people up to their rightful, original place, at the top of civilization.

At the end of the speech, to Malcolm's astonishment, Muhammad called him by name. He praised Malcolm in front of the whole gathering for his strength and faithfulness in prison.

After the meeting, Elijah Muhammad invited Wilfred and the whole family to dinner at his house.

Talking with Muhammad face to face, Malcolm marveled at the kind, gentle manner with which he spoke. Physically, the small, mild-mannered leader of the Nation of Islam was nothing like Malcolm's six-foot-four, domineering father. However, Malcolm felt that this man was his father in a spiritual sense, because he had given him a new life.

"Fishing" for the Nation of Islam

Malcolm was awed to be in Elijah Muhammad's presence, but he finally got up the courage to ask his advice. What was the best way to bring new members into the Detroit temple? "Go after the young people," answered Muhammad.

That was just what Malcolm wanted to know, and he returned to Detroit to launch a recruitment drive. After work, he spent all his spare time "fishing"—looking for new members for the Nation of Islam. He felt strengthened by the new name he had received from Elijah Muhammad—"Malcolm X."

Malcolm haunted the bars and poolrooms of the Detroit ghetto, looking for young men like his former self. He found plenty of them, but to his frustration, most of them were "too deaf, dumb, and blind, mentally, morally, and spiritually," to listen. Still, Malcolm worked so hard that he did bring in many new members. The size of Temple One tripled.

A Natural Speaker

The minister of the Detroit temple was impressed with Malcolm's powers of persuasion, and he asked him to share his personal experience of conversion to Islam, at meetings. Malcolm spoke to gatherings at the temple about how the Nation of Islam had turned his life around. He was such a forceful speaker, and he clearly knew so much about history and other subjects, that the minister then asked him to lecture at educational meetings.

Malcolm was eager to pass on everything he'd learned from reading. One of his favorite subjects was the horrors of the slave trade. Malcolm was determined to make African Americans understand how their forebears had come to this land. Although many whites had found freedom and opportunity in the Americas, blacks had found only a lifetime of servitude.

Malcolm was determined to make African Americans understand how their forebears had come to this land.

All their lives, for many generations, it had been drummed into African Americans that white was better, black was worse. The lighter the skin, the better. If only white people would accept black people, supposedly the problems of blacks would be solved.

Malcolm told his listeners that *blacks* were superior. He told them that blacks didn't need **integration** with whites and shouldn't even try for it. With a smile, he gave them one of his catchy slogans: "Coffee is the only thing I like integrated." (He took his coffee with cream.)

Malcolm got his points across with a rapid, punchy speaking style. His talks were peppered with memorable quotations. For instance, explaining why African Americans were different from all other Americans, he said, "We didn't land on Plymouth Rock, my brothers and sisters—Plymouth Rock landed on us!"

In the summer of 1953, not even a year after Malcolm was released from prison, he was appointed assistant minister of Temple One. The FBI noted his appointment in their records.

With soldiers needed for the Korean War, the draft board reviewed Malcolm's 4-F status and decided he was fit to serve

The Many Names of Malcolm X

Malcolm was named "Malcolm Little" by his parents, and he went by that name in school. He used it when he was with his sister Ella in Boston. In his life on the streets, Malcolm was called "Red" because of his bright red conked hair. In Charlestown State Prison, he was "prisoner number 22843."

As a member of the Nation of Islam, he became "Malcolm X," the name by which he is best known. Many members of the Nation of Islam took X as their new last name. They rejected their English last names, such as "Little" or "Sanders" (the original last name of the woman Malcolm eventually married). These English names were not their black ancestors' real names, but the names of slave owners. X is the letter of the alphabet that stands for the unknown, and therefore, it was fitting to have it stand for the lost names of the Africans who were kidnapped and forced into slavery in America.

Malcolm continued to use "Malcolm X" as his public name, but by 1959 he was using the Middle Eastern name "Malik Shabazz" on his driver's license and passport. "Shabazz" also became his wife's last name, and that of his daughters. Toward the end of Malcolm's life, after his pilgrimage—or spiritual journey—to Mecca, he often signed his letters "El Hajj Malik El-Shabazz." "El-Hajj" is a title that a Muslim may use after his pilgrimage is completed.

after all. FBI agents went to Malcolm's place of work to question him about why he hadn't registered for the draft. They also asked many questions about the Nation of Islam, and Malcolm sensed that this was their real concern. Because Elijah Muhammad advised his followers not to openly resist the draft, Malcolm did show up at his draft board, but he registered as a **conscientious objector**. At first the draft board accepted Malcolm's conscientious-objector standing, but after a psychiatric exam they reclassified him once more as 4-F, unfit for service.

"When the white man asked me to go off somewhere and fight and maybe die to preserve the way the white man treated the black man in America," Malcolm said sarcastically, "then my conscience made me object."

From his home in Chicago, Elijah Muhammad kept an eye on Brother Malcolm's progress, and he was most impressed. Malcolm was intelligent, he was a persuasive speaker, he followed Muhammad's teachings faithfully, and he was on fire to spread the word that had saved him. Muhammad invited Malcolm to Chicago several times for personal training.

Early in 1954, Elijah Muhammad decided that Malcolm was now ready for Boston. He sent him back there, with the mission to help grow the Nation of Islam.

Malcolm X, shown in this undated photograph at a civil rights demonstration, mesmerized listeners with his message and natural charm.

Anti-Communism and the Nation of Islam

After Germany and Japan were defeated in World War II, many Americans saw an even greater threat to Western democracy in the spread of communism. Led by the Soviet Union (USSR), the communist nations lined up against the United States and Western Europe. This struggle was called the cold war.

U.S. troops were fighting in Korea in the early 1950s, trying to prevent China from establishing a communist government there. At home, there was an atmosphere of fear and suspicion of anyone who criticized the United States. Because the Nation of Islam openly spoke against the government, claimed that African Americans weren't really citizens, and encouraged their members not to serve in the military, they were closely watched by the FBI. Their phones were tapped, they were followed, and spies within the NOI reported to the FBI.

This 1955 photo shows Richard M. Nixon, then vice president, examining evidence that would incriminate communist spy Alger Hiss. Like Hiss, the NOI was closely watched by the FBI.

CHAPTER 9

Spreading the Word

Much of what I say might sound like it's stirring up trouble, but it is the truth.

The Boston branch of the Nation of Islam, Temple Eleven, was so small at the beginning of 1954 that they met in a member's living room; but under Malcolm's leadership, the temple began to grow. In meeting after meeting, Brother Malcolm described slavery in graphic terms, blaming white people for "an orgy of greed and lust and murder."

Furthermore, even though white Boston thought of itself as the prime example of freedom-loving America, Malcolm pointed out the **hypocrisy** behind this myth. Some of the wealthiest men in Boston had made their fortunes in the slave trade.

Most of Malcolm's African American audience had never heard the past of their ancestors described this way or whites accused so bluntly. They were mesmerized.

Malcolm X in a 1963 photo, speaking to a NOI rally in Harlem. His pointing finger, as well as his words, accused whites of mistreating blacks.

Building the Nation of Islam

Malcolm had become a spellbinding speaker. The first time Ella went to Temple Eleven to hear him, she was transfixed. He spoke with a powerful rhythm, sweeping his audience along. "Much of what I say might sound bitter, but it's the truth. Much of what I say might sound like it's stirring up trouble, but it is the truth. Much of what I say might sound like it's hate, but it's the truth."

Malcolm's half sister Ella was one of the people in Boston whom Malcolm most wanted to bring into the Nation of Islam. Though she was awestruck at Malcolm's preaching, Ella had serious doubts about Elijah Muhammad's message. Still, she could see that Malcolm had turned his life around, as she had always hoped he would. She approved of the discipline and self-esteem that the Nation of Islam taught. Three years later, she would finally join Temple Eleven.

Within three months after Malcolm arrived, the Boston branch of the Nation of Islam was strong enough to open a storefront temple. Malcolm appointed Louis X (later Louis Farrakhan) as minister of the Boston temple. Malcolm then went on to Philadelphia, where the Nation of Islam temple was small, and the members were fighting among themselves. Again, he quickly organized the temple and attracted many new members. After only a few months, Philadelphia's Temple Twelve was firmly established.

Malcolm had become a spellbinding speaker.... He spoke with a powerful rhythm, sweeping his audience along.

Louis Farrakhan (b. 1933)

In the 1950s, Louis Walcott was a young professional musician and singer called The Charmer. He was converted to the Nation of Islam in 1955 when he heard Malcolm X preach at the Boston temple. As a member of the NOI, he took the name Louis X. He wrote the popular Nation of Islam song, "White Man's Heaven Is Black Man's Hell."

Malcolm X became Louis's mentor, or guide and teacher, and for years they were close friends. However, when Malcolm left the NOI in 1964, Louis publicly took Elijah Muhammad's side and condemned Malcolm. Louis X replaced Malcolm as minister of Temple Seven in New York. He later took on the last name of Farrakhan. A few years after Elijah Muhammad's death in 1975, Louis Farrakhan became the national minister of the Nation of Islam.

Under Louis Farrakhan's leadership, the Nation of Islam flourished and grew. In 1995, he led a demonstration called "The Million Man March." He is admired by many African Americans for his frank criticism of racism and for promoting black pride. However, he has also been widely criticized for his anti-Jewish statements.

Louis Farrakhan, also a powerful speaker, addresses an NOI group in this photo from the 1960s. In the late 1970s, Farrakhan became the new leader of the NOI.

Back to Harlem

With the Philadelphia temple in good shape, Elijah Muhammad sent Malcolm to New York in June 1954 to be the minister of the temple there. There were more than one million black people living in New York City, but only a small number of them belonged to the little storefront in Harlem that housed Temple Seven. This was a great opportunity for Minister Malcolm, and for the Nation of Islam.

Malcolm knew it wouldn't be easy to make converts in Harlem. From his years of street life there, he knew how tough and sophisticated New Yorkers were. There were preachers and political speakers of various kinds on every corner in Harlem, standing on their stepladders to be noticed. Most people paid them no attention.

This photo shows Malcolm X in Temple Seven, Harlem, c. 1965. By this time, the temple had its own restaurant, which served food prepared in accordance with Islamic law.

Malcolm spent his first few days walking and driving around Harlem, getting reacquainted with the place that had seemed like "seventh heaven" to him ten years ago. Now he saw Harlem with different eyes. He saw the dealers selling drugs, the addicts using them, and the prostitutes meeting customers in broad daylight. He saw the police looking on as if all this law-breaking had nothing to do with them.

Malcolm looked for friends from his old days in Harlem, including Sammy and West Indian Archie. Sammy was dead. West Indian Archie was almost worse than dead—a pathetic, sick old man. If Malcolm hadn't been saved by the Nation of Islam, he knew, he'd be either dead or a washed-up wreck himself.

Malcolm's Recruiting Methods

Seeing what had happened to his old friends made Malcolm more determined than ever to spread Elijah Muhammad's message. He used many different tactics to lure people to the lectures at Temple Seven. He and his helpers passed out handbills, often on the edges of groups that gathered to listen to black nationalists. Those people, already interested in the idea of black independence, would be more likely to come to a Nation of Islam meeting.

Malcolm was especially pleased with his idea of waiting outside Christian churches in Harlem on Sunday mornings. When the congregation came out, Malcolm was there to invite the people to the Nation of Islam Sunday afternoon service. Coming from a black Baptist family, Malcolm knew how precious their religion was to these churchgoers. If he could only make them see that the natural religion for black people was Islam!

"Brothers and sisters," Malcolm told the people as they left church, "the white man has brainwashed us black people to fasten our gaze upon a blond-haired, blue-eyed Jesus!" It was a shocking pronouncement, but sometimes it made them rethink their religion.

For those who joined Temple Seven, Malcolm offered a full program. Monday night, the Fruit of Islam (FOI) trained. The Fruit of Islam—so called because the fruit of a tree is both the final product and the beginning of a new tree—was the private police branch for the NOI. They served as bodyguards for Elijah Muhammad and other leaders. The boys and young men in the FOI were drilled by captains and taught tactics and the use of firearms. The FOI trainees also heard lectures on such topics as personal hygiene, how to become a responsible husband and father, and sound business principles.

The Fruit of Islam...was the private police branch for the NOI.

Tuesday was Unity Night, for men and women members of the temple to socialize. Wednesday night, the temple offered

In this photo, members of the Fruit of Islam lock arms, preparing for Louis Farrakhan's arrival at the Millions More Movement rally in Washington, D.C., in 2005.

classes in the basic beliefs of Islam. Thursday night—for women and girls—was Muslim Girls' Training and General Civilization Class. In Elijah Muhammad's teaching, women needed special instruction in cooking, sewing, childcare, and proper behavior. Friday was Civilization Night, when men and women learned how to be good husbands and wives according to Muslim practice. Saturday night was free.

A Spellbinding Speaker

Sunday, when the temple held worship services, was Malcolm's chance to draw in new members with his natural gift for public speaking. Reading constantly and gathering more material, he worked hard to develop his gift. He studied other powerful orators to learn their techniques. He learned from his reading of Cicero, the most famous orator of ancient Rome, that

Malcolm X is photographed speaking at an outdoor rally in Harlem in 1963.

touching people's emotions was more persuasive than rational arguments. He watched Billy Graham, the world-famous evangelical Christian preacher, and saw how he got the audience involved in his speeches.

As a public speaker, Malcolm had an intense relationship with his audience. Large groups of people listened as if he were speaking to each one personally. He spoke with such passion that sometimes his shirt would be soaked with perspiration by the end of the speech.

Malcolm's black audiences were thrilled to hear him speak, without any sugarcoating, about how whites denied them their human rights. Also, they loved the figure Malcolm presented. Here was a tall, handsome black man, intelligent and well spoken, with a proud, fearless bearing, declaring openly what most black people hardly dared to think. Here was a hero for them.

National Successes

While Temple Seven was growing, Malcolm also traveled to other cities to establish Nation of Islam groups and help them grow. Malcolm was driven by his belief that every black person in America would join the Nation of Islam, if they understood their situation clearly. He had boundless energy, and he didn't need much sleep.

Malcolm opened temples in Brooklyn and Queens, New York; in Hartford, Connecticut; and in Springfield, Massachusetts. Temples in New Jersey, Pennsylvania, Florida, Ohio, Virginia, and Georgia followed.

By 1956, tens of thousands of black Americans had joined the Nation of Islam. Elijah Muhammad was greatly pleased with Malcolm's success.

CHAPTER 10

Showing Black Power

No black man should have that much power.
—*Editor James L. Hicks*
of the New York Amsterdam News

One theme Malcolm X stressed again and again in his speeches was the foolishness of black people trying to integrate with white people. Why would they want to integrate with the whites who had mistreated them so badly? He pointed out how hypocritical northern whites were, pretending that race problems were all in the South. Malcolm had grown up in the North and lived there all his life—mainly in the ghettos of Boston, New York, and Detroit. "Ultra-liberal New York had more integration problems than Mississippi," he said.

Besides, why would African Americans want to integrate with a race that was on its way out? Elijah Muhammad taught that the white race was weak, corrupt—and doomed. When black people realized how they had been brainwashed and cheated, they would naturally take control. Instead of returning to Africa, as Marcus Garvey had taught, they would establish their own black nation in America. Their ancestors had toiled and suffered on this land for hundreds of years, and they deserved their own territory here.

Malcolm was continually adding information to his lectures from his reading. One of his favorite haunts in Harlem was the National Memorial African Bookstore on

The National Memorial African Book Store was a favorite haunt of Malcolm's. In this 1964 photo, he gives a press conference in the bookstore office.

Seventh Avenue at 125th Street. He became friends with the owner, Louis Michaux, and used the store as his personal library. Malcolm spent so much time at Michaux's that people who wanted to contact him called and left messages for him there. Because the bookstore was a magnet for people interested in black nationalism, Malcolm sometimes gave speeches in front of the store.

An Example of Black Power

Among his many activities, Malcolm helped choose and train young men for the Fruit of Islam. A **stereotype** that many white people held about blacks was that they were undisciplined, lazy, and cowardly. Members of the Nation of Islam were proud to present themselves as just the opposite: disciplined, hard working, and brave. Unusually strong, dedicated young men, the Fruit of Islam police members underwent special training in martial arts, such as karate, and military tactics.

In 1957, an incident in Harlem brought the Nation of Islam into the national news. One night in April, two white policemen broke up a street fight in Harlem. Johnson Hinton, one of the onlookers, protested when the police officers started beating a drunken man. One of the police officers ordered Hinton to move on. Later, the officer and Hinton gave differing accounts as to whether Hinton did start to leave or refused to leave. In any case, the officers beat him severely and took him away to the nearest police station on 123rd Street.

The incident wasn't unusual in Harlem, except that Johnson Hinton was a member of the Nation of Islam. Word spread quickly, and within half an hour Malcolm and fifty of the Fruit of Islam, all in dark suits and ties, stood in ranks in front of the 123rd Street station. An angry black crowd gathered behind them. Malcolm demanded to see Brother Hinton.

Members of the Nation of Islam were proud to present themselves as just the opposite: disciplined, hard working, and brave.

At first the police refused to allow Malcolm to come into the station. When they finally let him in, Malcolm found Hinton bleeding and barely conscious. Malcolm demanded that Hinton be taken to Harlem Hospital. He and the Fruit of Islam troops marched the fifteen blocks, following the ambulance, to the amazement of everyone who saw them.

An even larger crowd gathered at the hospital, and the city authorities were afraid there would be a riot. Malcolm promised to disperse the crowd on the condition that Hinton receive medical treatment. When the police agreed, he made one motion of his arm—and both the Fruit of Islam men and the black crowd melted away. "No man should have that much power," a white official commented. Reporting the incident in the black newspaper *New York Amsterdam News*, the editor James L. Hicks wrote that it was clear the official meant, "No *black* man should have that much power."

With this dramatic demonstration of disciplined strength, the Nation of Islam and Malcolm X gained national attention in the black community. Elijah Muhammad appointed Malcolm as his national representative.

A Mutual Attraction

Many young women in the Nation of Islam were already very interested in Minister Malcolm as a good-looking, personable leader—and perhaps as a husband. However, Malcolm, working and traveling constantly to build up the movement, had no time for socializing. In any case, the Nation of Islam did not encourage men and women to socialize much. The sexes were separated in school, and they sat apart in audiences.

Betty Sanders, later known as Betty Shabazz, was photographed here in 1972, several years after Malcolm's death. She raised their six children and continued her education, earning a PhD in 1975, and then taught at Medgar Evers College in New York.

After hearing Minister Malcolm speak in 1956, a young nursing student named Betty Sanders decided to join Temple Seven and become Betty X. It wasn't so much what the tall, lean preacher said as his air of natural dignity and strength. She was intensely drawn to him.

Betty felt that the minister needed someone to take care of him. Malcolm was thin, almost gaunt, and there were dark circles under his eyes. "This man is totally malnourished," she said to herself. "He needs some liver, some spinach, some beets, and broccoli."

The attraction was not one-sided. Malcolm noticed her as well. She was dark-skinned, brown-eyed, and very pretty. She was also intelligent and college-educated. Although Malcolm did not court Betty in a romantic way, he found himself spending more time with Sister Betty. As the minister, he would drop in on the hygiene classes she was teaching for Nation of Islam women and girls. On one occasion, Malcolm asked Betty to come along on an educational outing to the Museum of Natural History. However, he still kept telling himself that he was too busy to get married.

In fact, Malcolm had decided it was time for the Nation of Islam to put out its own newspaper. He had been writing a column, "God's Angry Men," for the *New York Amsterdam News* and other African American newspapers. While in Los Angeles to organize a temple there, he studied the operations of the *Los Angeles Herald Dispatch*, a black newspaper. Late in 1957,

In 1957, Malcolm X started the newspaper *Muhammad Speaks*. This 1964 photo shows a member of the NOI outside the Coliseum in Chicago, Illinois, selling the paper with Elijah Muhammad's image on the front page.

with the help of black journalist Louis Lomax, he started to publish *Muhammad Speaks* in Harlem.

Elijah Muhammad was pleased with the newspaper, yet he still urged Malcolm to choose a wife. He thought it would set a good example for other members of the Nation of Islam, and he thought it would be good for Malcolm.

Marriage

Malcolm agreed it was time for him to get married. Everyone, including Muhammad, seemed to think Sister Betty was a good choice. Yet the prospect of actually getting married made Malcolm very, very nervous. He thought of his parents' unhappy marriage, and he thought of all the untrustworthy women he had known in his street life. Women were weak, he thought. Women were vain. Women talked too much.

Unable to talk himself completely out of marriage, Malcolm stopped at a gas station while in Michigan and called Betty from a pay phone. "Look," he blurted out, "do you want to get married?" Although Betty had known that Malcolm was interested in her, she screamed with excitement and dropped the phone. She then caught the first plane to Detroit, where they were married on January 14, 1958. He was thirty-two, and she was twenty-three. They celebrated with dinner at Philbert's house in Lansing.

Malcolm thought the sentimental notions encouraged by Hollywood movies had nothing to do with real married love. However, he needed a wife's support, and he trusted Betty. He told his biographer, Alex Haley, "She's one of the very few—four women—whom I have ever trusted."

In November 1958, their first child, Attallah, was born. As it turned out, Malcolm's trust in Betty was well founded. For all of

Malcolm X, photographed here with his daughters Attalah (right) and Qubilah (left).

their life together, she devoted herself to being his wife and the mother of his children.

Throughout Malcolm and Betty's marriage, Malcolm spent much of his time traveling. Even when he was home, he worked long hours. In 1958, shortly after Malcolm and Betty married, Elijah Muhammad sent Malcolm X on a three-week trip to Africa and the Middle East.

White Americans were mostly unaware of the Nation of Islam, but across the Atlantic Ocean, the newly independent African countries took a keen interest in the movement. Malcolm was welcomed in Egypt, Arabia, Sudan, Nigeria, and Ghana as the representative of Elijah Muhammad and the Nation of Islam.

African Nationalism

In the nineteenth century, European nations competed to seize territory in Africa, until together they controlled most of the continent. Liberia alone, established by freed slaves, had been independent since 1847. After World War II, black Africans began to shake off European **colonialism** and struggled toward self-rule.

Morocco became independent from France in 1956. In 1957, Ghana became independent from Great Britain. In 1960, Nigeria followed suit. Algeria achieved independence from France in 1962. These African countries that had freed themselves from European domination felt a natural kinship with the black nationalist movement in the United States.

A crowd cheers election results in this photo taken in Lagos, Nigeria, December 16, 1959. Nigeria achieved independence from Great Britain the next year.

CHAPTER 11

The Growth of Two Movements

What is looked upon as an American dream for white people has long been an American nightmare for black people.

When Malcolm was paroled from prison in 1952, the Nation of Islam had numbered only a few hundred. Under Malcolm's leadership, the organization had grown to tens of thousands by the late 1950s. The Nation of Islam no longer needed to meet in living rooms or even in storefronts. They began to hold big rallies in major cities. They rented sports arenas for thousands of faithful members and thousands of other black people who came to hear Elijah Muhammad speak in New York, Chicago, and Washington, D.C.

White people were not allowed at these meetings. To Malcolm's amusement, some of them complained that the Nation of Islam was practicing segregation. "Accusing *us* of segregation!" he exclaimed. "Across the nation, whites barring blacks was standard."

At the rallies, Malcolm was often the speaker who introduced Muhammad, the Nation of Islam's spiritual leader. There would be tears in his eyes as he gazed at the small, slight man. "America's wisest black man!" he told the cheering audience. "America's boldest black man!

America's most fearless black man! This wilderness of North America's most powerful black man!"

"The Hate That Hate Produced"

At the beginning of 1959, most white people had never heard of the Nation of Islam. However, that was about to change. That spring the journalist Louis Lomax asked Malcolm X if he would be willing to be interviewed for a TV documentary on the Nation of Islam. It would be shown by the CBS network on the popular *Mike Wallace Show*. At first, Malcolm was not in favor of cooperating with the TV producers. When Elijah Muhammad decided it was a good idea, Malcolm agreed.

When the program was aired that July, it was titled "The Hate That Hate Produced." Like the title, the program aimed to shock and frighten. It emphasized the anti-white teachings of the Nation of Islam, without describing the hundreds of years of white oppression. It presented the Nation of Islam as militant black racists.

Malcolm was angry but not surprised. As one reporter after another called to get his reaction, he let them have it. "For the white man to ask the black man if he hates him is just like the rapist asking the raped, or the wolf asking the sheep, 'Do you hate me?' The white man is in no moral position to accuse anyone else of hate!"

Suddenly everyone in America knew about the Nation of Islam. Whites who viewed the documentary were shocked to hear Malcolm X state that the evil serpent in the Garden of Eden, in the Bible, was actually a symbol for the white man. They were offended to hear themselves described as "blond-haired, pale-skinned, blue-and green-eyed devils," an inferior race destined to be wiped out. They were frightened to see thousands of organized, disciplined black men and women applauding as Malcolm X talked about the destruction of the "wicked white race in the war of Armageddon."

Shortly after the program had introduced Americans to the Nation of Islam, a book titled *The Black Muslims in America* was published. The author was a respected black sociologist, C. Eric Lincoln. His book was a scholarly, evenhanded study of the NOI. However, the main idea that readers seemed to pick up from the book was the name "Black Muslims." Malcolm protested over and over that members of the Nation of Islam were simply "Muslims," but the name stuck.

Malcolm in the Limelight

Malcolm X and others in the Nation of Islam felt that "The Hate That Hate Produced" was an unfair portrait of their organization. Even so, it resulted in more publicity. Widely read magazines such as *Time*, *Newsweek*, *Life*, and *The Reader's Digest* all ran stories on the Nation of Islam. The membership surged.

Some whites were curious to learn more about the organization, and Malcolm was invited to speak at many colleges and universities. Professors and students alike were impressed with how well educated Malcolm was, although he had only finished the eighth grade in school. He had an excellent memory and could quote from the Bible and the Quran—the holy book of Islam—at length.

This open copy of the Quran is written in Arabic, the common language of Islam.

Malcolm enjoyed these appearances. "It was like being on a battlefield," he said, "with intellectual and philosophical bullets." Speaking at Boston University, he told the mostly white audience that he wasn't being disrespectful when he told them what black people really thought; he was just being frank. Blacks who wanted integration, he said, would tell whites what they wanted to hear to get "some of the crumbs that you might let fall from your table. Well, I'm not looking for crumbs, so I'm not trying to delude you."

Controversy Among Black Leaders

White commentators called Malcolm X a hatemonger, a racist **demagogue**, and his followers black supremacists. Some black leaders agreed, and they feared that the Nation of Islam would only hurt race relations. Roy Wilkins of the National Association for the Advancement of Colored People (NAACP) announced, "The NAACP opposes and regards as dangerous any group, white or black, political or religious, that preaches hatred among men." He did add pointedly, "The so-called Muslims who teach black supremacy and hatred of all white people have gained a following only because America has been so slow in granting equal opportunities and has permitted the abuse and persecution of Negro citizens."

White commentators called Malcolm X a hatemonger . . .

Malcolm X scorned Roy Wilkins as the kind of black "leader" who spent all his time with white people and had no idea what most black people wanted. "Every time I've seen Roy Wilkins," said Malcolm, "he's been at the Waldorf." (The Waldorf is one of New York's most luxurious hotels.)

On the other hand, many black people who watched the program were drawn to the Nation of Islam. These were mainly poor people, leading a miserable existence in crime-ridden slums. They weren't willing to wait for the slow, patient methods of the NAACP, or even the civil rights movement, to take effect. They could see how the Nation of Islam changed its members' lives for the better—*right away*. As George S. Schuyler from the *Pittsburgh Courier*, a black newspaper, wrote, "Mr. Muhammad may be a rogue and a charlatan, but when anybody can get tens of thousands of Negroes to practice economic solidarity, respect their women, alter their atrocious diet, give up liquor, stop crime, juvenile delinquency and adultery, he is doing more for the Negro's welfare than any current leader I know."

Roy Wilkins, executive secretary of the NAACP, is shown in this 1963 photo. After several frustrating public debates with Malcolm, Wilkins avoided appearing with him.

The Civil Rights Movement

The publicity for the Nation of Islam also gave a boost to the career of another black leader, Martin Luther King, Jr. Unlike Malcolm X with his fiery talk of self-defense for blacks against the "white devils," Martin Luther King, Jr., instructed his followers to love their enemies, and to resist injustice with nonviolence. King might embarrass whites and make them feel guilty, but he didn't alarm them the way Malcolm X did.

In the mid-1950s, the civil rights movement had started to come to the national attention. Many black Americans (as well as liberal whites) pinned their hopes on a better way of life through integration and equal opportunity for all. King, a young preacher at that time, led a boycott of the city buses in Montgomery, Alabama, demanding equal treatment for its black riders. The civil rights movement slowly gained momentum.

In 1960, the civil rights movement staged a series of "sit-ins." In several different southern cities, black students would sit down at a segregated lunch counter in a store such as Woolworth's. They were not served, and they were often taunted or even attacked, but they remained seated until they were arrested or the store closed.

These demonstrations gained attention and sympathy from many Americans for the civil rights cause, but Malcolm scoffed at the very goal of integration. Because the civil rights movement had support from liberal whites, he termed Martin Luther King, Jr., "a professional Negro," by which he meant, "His profession is being a Negro for the white man." He also called King an "Uncle Tom"—a belittling reference to a black character in the nineteenth-century novel *Uncle Tom's Cabin*. This famous book had brought the problems of slavery before the public and aided the anti-slavery cause around the time of the Civil War.

Martin Luther King, Jr., photographed at a press conference in 1964. Although Malcolm criticized King publicly, he liked and admired him.

The Montgomery Bus Boycott

On December 1, 1955, Rosa **Parks**, a black workingwoman, refused to give up her seat on a city bus to a white passenger. The bus driver had her arrested for breaking a Montgomery law that upheld segregation in public transportation and required blacks to give up their seats to whites. She was convicted and fined, but Rosa Parks's action sparked a citywide bus boycott by black riders that lasted more than a year. The boycott brought national attention to the segregation problem and launched the civil rights movement. Martin Luther King, Jr., was propelled into the national headlines and became the most eloquent speaker for civil rights.

This photo shows Rosa Parks in the *front* of a bus in Montgomery, Alabama, on December 21, 1956, after the boycott had forced the city to change its segregationist law.

Civil Rights and President Kennedy

Meanwhile, the civil rights movement continued to grow. In 1960, John F. Kennedy was elected president. It was a very close election, and Kennedy owed his victory partly to the support of black voters. Since his election, Kennedy took some actions to support the cause of civil rights. When African American James Meredith became the first black student at the University of

African American college students are photographed during a sit-in at a Woolworth's lunch counter in Greensboro, North Carolina, February 2, 1960. Malcolm scorned their goal of "a desegregated cup of coffee."

Mississippi in 1962, the president sent federal marshals to protect him while he enrolled.

Malcolm X thought President Kennedy should have done much more. For instance, Kennedy had waited two years to sign an executive order forbidding **racial discrimination** in housing financed by the U.S. government. Malcolm was not impressed by the president's symbolic gestures toward racial equality, such as the choice of the black singer Marian Anderson to sing the national anthem at his inauguration.

In June 1963 President Kennedy announced that he would ask Congress to enact laws to ensure racial equality in America. Although the speech was hailed by many civil rights leaders as a great advance, Malcolm was scornful. He called President Kennedy's speech "mealy-mouthed." He pointed out that the president had not sent troops to Birmingham, Alabama, in April to protect civil rights demonstrators from violence. It was not until riots broke out after the demonstrations that the president finally sent troops.

Uncle Tom's Cabin

Harriet Beecher Stowe's novel *Uncle Tom's Cabin*, published in 1852, awakened white Americans to the horrors of slavery in their own country. Through the story of Uncle Tom, an enslaved black man of almost Christ-like goodness, the book vividly described the desperate lives of African Americans. *Uncle Tom's Cabin* sold millions of copies, and many whites turned against slavery as a result of reading it. A century later, Malcolm X read the book in prison and learned much about slavery from it.

This poster for a play based on the 1852 novel shows the characters Uncle Tom and Eva. Stage versions of *Uncle Tom's Cabin* often featured demeaning racial stereotypes of blacks.

Although the character of Uncle Tom in the book is courageous as well as saintly, Malcolm X and other black nationalists ridiculed him for suffering without fighting back. The name "Uncle Tom" came to be an insult, meaning a black man who is subservient to white people.

The March on Washington

That same summer in 1963, leaders of the civil rights movement planned a demonstration called the March on Washington for Jobs and Freedom. The idea was to show America that racial harmony was possible. The demonstrators gathered on August 28, 1963, on the Mall in Washington, D.C. They marched from the Washington Monument to the Lincoln Memorial, where Martin Luther King, Jr., gave a stirring speech.

The participants numbered more than 200,000—a quarter of them white. They marched peacefully, singing "We Shall Overcome." Americans across the country watched the event on TV, and many were deeply moved.

Malcolm watched the March on Washington as an observer, but he was not impressed with King's dream. As he said, "What is looked upon as an American dream for white people has long been an American nightmare for black people." He called the demonstration a "Farce on Washington." He wasn't surprised when, only two weeks after the March on Washington, white

This photo shows the March on Washington, August 28, 1963. Many in the Kennedy administration feared that the march would turn violent.

"I Have a Dream"

The highlight of the 1963 March on Washington was Martin Luther King, Jr.,'s "I have a dream" speech. Standing in front of the Lincoln Memorial, he reminded the audience of the great hope aroused by the Emancipation Proclamation one hundred years earlier. He pointed out how shameful it was that black Americans were still not truly free, but "crippled by the manacles of segregation and the chains of discrimination." As King described his vision for a future when black children and white children would naturally join hands "as sisters and brothers," he repeated over and over the phrase, "I have a dream." The listening crowd swayed and shouted with the rhythm of his voice.

Martin Luther King, Jr., was photographed giving his "I have a dream" speech to a rapt audience. This famous speech captured the hopes and dreams of many African Americans.

racists bombed a black church in Birmingham, Alabama. Four girls were killed.

In November 1963, Malcolm spoke at a large rally in Detroit. The audience was mainly black, but also mainly non-Muslim. "We have a common enemy," he said. He went on to talk about revolution, linking African Americans' struggle for freedom with the struggle for freedom of colonized peoples in Africa and Asia.

Malcolm mocked the civil rights movement as "the only revolution in which the goal is a desegregated lunch counter, a desegregated theater, a desegregated park and a desegregated public toilet; you can sit down next to white folks—on the toilet." The proper goal of African Americans, he urged, was their own land—a separate nation.

On September 15, 1963, the Sixteenth Street Baptist Church in Birmingham, Alabama, was bombed. In this photo taken the next day, a somber crowd of African Americans watches FBI bomb experts searching the rubble.

Face of the NOI

The Honorable Elijah Muhammad teaches that for the black man in America the only solution is complete separation from the white man.

Malcolm was busier than ever. Sometimes he traveled so much that he was home only twice a month. However, when he was home, he cherished his time with his family. Malcolm and Betty now had two more girls besides Attallah: Qubilah, born in 1960; and Ilyasah, born in 1962.

Malcolm might be a celebrity in the outside world, but at home he was "Daddy." His three little daughters would pounce on him when he came in the door and try to climb into his lap all at once. He loved to play games with them, giggle with them, and read to them.

Sometimes Malcolm would turn on the television to watch himself on the

On May 21, 1964, Malcolm X was photographed just off the plane from his journey to Mecca. He holds his daughter Ilyasah, who years later would write *Growing Up X* about her life as Malcolm's daughter.

news. The children would stare in amazement, looking from the Daddy in the living room to the Daddy on the TV screen. They went up to the TV to take a close look, then ran back to the real Daddy. Malcolm and Betty would laugh.

A Dutiful Wife

Although Betty had graduated from college and trained for the profession of nursing, she followed the Nation of Islam's teaching about a wife's proper role. According to Elijah Muhammad, a man was supposed to protect his wife and children and provide for them. A woman was supposed to focus her life on running the home and raising the children. In public, Muhammad taught, a woman should be quiet and retiring, always modestly dressed.

Betty saw her mission in life as supporting Malcolm's mission. Besides ironing his shirts and pressing his trousers, she helped him with his work. She typed and proofread his speeches and newspaper columns, answered phone calls, and entertained visiting ministers from other cities, such as Louis X from Boston.

Betty saw her mission in life as supporting Malcolm's mission.

Betty kept Malcolm well fed with healthy home cooking, including homemade bread. She kept their home peaceful and happy, a haven for him to return to. In most areas, Betty trusted Malcolm's judgment and obeyed his wishes.

However, Betty sometimes worried about the family's financial security. Malcolm didn't own a house or a car, and he had no savings or life insurance. How could she support the family if something happened to her husband? He assured her that the Nation of Islam would take care of them.

Debating the Race Issue

Malcolm's work in the late 1950s and the early 1960s included a round of debates on radio and television shows. He was scornful of anyone, black or white, who believed that integration was the answer to America's race problems. He stated, "The Honorable Elijah Muhammad teaches that for the black man in America the only solution is complete separation from the white man."

Speaking rapidly and forcefully, Malcolm bowled his debate opponents over. "My technique is nonstop, until what I want to get said is said." Malcolm knew all the arguments his opponents would use against him, and he was ready for them.

This undated photo shows Malcolm speaking at a rally. He often scorned the idea of integration and described it as a trick by whites to keep blacks enslaved.

When anyone suggested that Malcolm was trying to "incite Negroes to violence," he would remind his listeners about the endless violence that African Americans had suffered from white people. "It is a miracle that the American black people have remained a peaceful people." If someone accused the Nation of Islam of not supporting the U.S. government, Malcolm would shoot back, "Does the government support and protect us?"

Even though Malcolm X was now the public face of the Nation of Islam, he was always careful to speak of Elijah

Muhammad as the prophet and leader of the movement. All his speeches and writings were peppered with "Mr. Muhammad says . . ." and "The Honorable Elijah Muhammad teaches . . ." He believed that Elijah Muhammad was literally the divine Messenger of Allah, that he had saved Malcolm's life for a higher purpose, and that he could save every black person in America if they would only listen to his message. Malcolm intended to make them listen.

Jealousy in the Ranks

By the early 1960s, Malcolm X had become the chief spokesman for the Nation of Islam. The media often referred to Malcolm as "the Number Two Black Muslim," although Malcolm patiently explained that there wasn't any "Number Two," only Number One—Elijah Muhammad. By this time, Elijah Muhammad was suffering from severe asthma, and he was not able to make many public appearances. He finally moved to Arizona, a better climate for his health than Illinois.

Ever since his conversion in prison, Malcolm X had been devoted to Elijah Muhammad like a son devoted to his father. Muhammad, in turn, had treated Malcolm like a favored son. Early on in Malcolm's career with the Nation of Islam, Elijah Muhammad had warned him of envy. "You will grow to be hated when you become well known."

. . . Elijah Muhammad had warned him of envy. "You will grow to be hated when you become well known."

Now Malcolm realized that his leader's prediction was coming true. He had bitter enemies among the officials of the Nation of Islam. The NOI had grown into a large, wealthy organization, and so there was a great deal at stake over who would control it. Also, Elijah Muhammad's bad health made his assistants wonder how much longer he could control the Nation of Islam, and who would inherit his power.

Malcolm did have honest differences of opinion with other leaders in the NOI. Elijah Muhammad and his closest lieutenants wanted to avoid direct conflict with white society. Muhammad discouraged his followers from getting involved with the civil rights movement, and he wanted Malcolm to tone down his fiery speeches. Malcolm tried to obey Muhammad, but

Elijah Muhammad shown at the podium in a 1964 photo. In spite of severe asthma, Muhammad continued to lead the NOI until his death in 1975.

he did attend some civil rights demonstrations. Although Malcolm scorned the goal of integration, he thought the NOI should show approval for any civil rights actions against injustice to African Americans.

Meanwhile, members of Muhammad's family and other officials in the organization, such as the supreme captain of the Fruit of Islam, Raymond Sharieff, and the national secretary, John Ali, were resentful of Malcolm's fame. Muhammad's son Herbert, now editor of the NOI newspaper, *Muhammad Speaks*, stopped printing any news about Malcolm X. Rumors began to circulate in the Nation of Islam that Malcolm intended to take over the organization.

No Riches

It was also rumored that Malcolm had grown rich at the Nation's expense. In fact, Malcolm X did not own any property and was not wealthy. He liked to say that his only belongings were his glasses, his watch, and his briefcase. The car he drove belonged to the Nation of Islam; the seven-room brick house where he and his family lived in Queens, New York, was owned by the Nation of Islam. He had no savings in the bank.

Malcolm's half sister Ella, who had always been a sharp money manager, worried about Malcolm's finances. She felt concerned that while Elijah Muhammad was taking steps to ensure his own financial security, Malcom was not doing enough to secure funds for himself and his family's future. Malcolm couldn't stand to hear his leader criticized. Such remarks upset him so much that he wouldn't call or visit Ella for weeks.

But more and more, Malcolm felt unappreciated by Elijah Muhammad's inner circle of officials. Malcolm worked tirelessly, sometimes eighteen or twenty hours a day, for the Nation of Islam. He had never taken more than a small living allowance from the funds he sent to NOI headquarters in Chicago. Other Nation of Islam leaders owned luxurious houses and expensive cars and had fat bank accounts. Malcolm owned nothing.

Elijah Muhammad Exposed

While tension was growing in the top ranks of the NOI in 1962, Malcolm discovered disturbing facts about Elijah Muhammad. Although Muhammad preached strict sexual morality for his followers, he allegedly had sexual relations with several of his young women secretaries. Some of them had children by him. Apparently Muhammad, who punished others—

including Malcolm's brother Reginald—for the sin of adultery, was an adulterer himself.

Furthermore, Malcolm began to question some of the decisions made by Elijah Muhammad and those at NOI headquarters in Chicago. On April 27, 1962, violence broke out between the Nation of Islam and the Los Angeles police department. Two members of the temple there were stopped by a patrol car and questioned. One of them was severely beaten, and the other was shot to death.

. . . Malcolm discovered disturbing facts about Elijah Muhammad.

Many men in the Los Angeles temple were ready to start a war against all the whites in America. Malcolm, too, was full of rage, and he thought the NOI should at least take legal action against the Los Angeles police. Elijah Muhammad, in spite of preaching that the white authorities were doomed, did not want open conflict with them. The Nation of Islam was to keep to itself and leave the vengeance to Allah. On Muhammad's orders, Malcolm flew to Los Angeles and calmed down the young NOI men who wanted vengeance now.

Following an altercation between NOI members and the Los Angeles police, Malcolm used his speaking skills to prevent a full-scale riot there. A persuasive speaker, Malcolm is pictured here in a c. 1960 photo giving a speech.

In spite of his private doubts, Malcolm continued to praise Elijah Muhammad in his speeches and give him credit for everything the Nation of Islam had accomplished. When Alex Haley, a journalist, asked Malcolm if he could write a book about his life, Malcolm told him to get Elijah Muhammad's permission first. Muhammad did give permission, and Malcolm's first dictation to Haley was the biography's dedication: to "the Honorable Elijah Muhammad" who "made me the man I am today."

Alex Haley, writer of Malcolm X's autobiography, photographed c. 1988. Haley is best known as the author of the book *Roots*, made into an extremely popular TV miniseries in 1977.

Malcolm struggled against believing that Elijah Muhammad, his spiritual father, had actually committed the sin of adultery, but finally he could no longer deny the evidence. In April 1963 he visited Muhammad and asked him face to face how he could justify his behavior. Muhammad could not justify it, except to claim that it had been ordained by Allah that he would behave like David, the great but adulterous king of ancient Israel.

CHAPTER 13

A New Outlook

[There was a] spirit of unity and brotherhood that my experiences in America had led me to believe never could exist between the white and the non-white.

On November 22, 1963, President John F. Kennedy was shot by an assassin in Dallas, Texas. The nation was plunged into shock and grief. Malcolm, when asked for his reaction by reporters, said it was a case of "the chickens

President John F. Kennedy and his wife, Jacqueline, are shown in this photograph in Dallas, Texas, on November 22, 1963, moments before the president was assassinated.

coming home to roost." What he meant was that the hate Americans had for black people had spread throughout society, and finally the same violence that whites showed toward blacks had now killed their own leader, the president.

However, from the way the media reported Malcolm's comment, it sounded as if Malcolm—and the Nation of Islam— were glad that President Kennedy had been shot.

Malcolm Is Silenced

Elijah Muhammad had already warned all the leaders in the Nation of Islam not to comment at all on President Kennedy's assassination. If a reporter asked, they were supposed to say, "No comment." Every member of the Nation of Islam, including the highest officials, was supposed to follow Muhammad's instructions to the letter. When Malcolm X went to Chicago the next day to meet with Elijah Muhammad, he was very displeased. He told Malcolm that because he had disobeyed and had spoken to the press, he was now silenced—he would not be allowed to speak for the Nation of Islam for ninety days.

Being silenced for three months was a harsh punishment for Malcolm X. Speaking was what he did best, and he knew he was a powerful preacher and defender for the Nation of Islam. He felt that no other leader

Malcolm X and Muhammad Ali were photographed in Miami on January 1, 1964. Before he took the name "Muhammad Ali," the heavyweight champ was known as Cassius Clay.

could handle public relations for the Nation of Islam as well as he did. However, he submitted to the punishment. He told the media that he would not be speaking in public for ninety days.

With a heavy heart, Malcolm took this time for a vacation. In early 1964, his boxer friend Cassius Clay invited Malcolm and his family to stay with him in Miami, where he was training for a big fight. During this visit, Malcolm X persuaded Clay to join the Nation of Islam.

Breaking with the NOI

While Malcolm was in Miami, he began to realize that he would not be allowed to resume leadership in the Nation of Islam. Elijah Muhammad's spokesmen began to hint that Malcolm had "rebelled" against Muhammad, and for Black Muslims, disobedience toward Muhammad was the worst sin imaginable.

Therefore, Malcolm's silencing would last even longer than three months. He would not be allowed to teach, even in his own temple. In fact, it seemed that his enemies intended to force him out of the Nation of Islam entirely. Malcolm was shaken to his core. He knew that some officials in the Nation of Islam hated him. Yet how could Elijah Muhammad, the man he regarded as his spiritual father, the man he would have died for, betray him like this? "My head felt like it was bleeding inside," he said. "I felt like my brain was damaged."

Malcolm had to face the fact that the Nation of Islam, which had been his community, his church, and his home for eleven years, had rejected him. Even his brothers and sisters and closest friends shunned him—except for Ella. His brother Philbert publicly denounced him, calling him a traitor like Judas or Benedict Arnold.

Muhammad Ali (b. 1942)

In February 1964, Cassius Clay was scheduled to fight Sonny Liston for the title of world heavyweight boxing champion. Before his fight, Cassius Clay amused boxing fans by boasting that he would "float like a butterfly, sting like a bee." After he won the fight and the title, Clay announced that he was now a member of the Nation of Islam. Later, he took the new name that Elijah Muhammad gave him, "Muhammad Ali."

Ali claimed conscientious-objector status as a member of the Nation of Islam during the Vietnam War. As a result, he was barred from boxing in the United States, but he continued to box abroad. Ali converted to mainstream Islam in 1975.

A three-time world heavyweight champion, Muhammad Ali became a symbol of proud black manhood for many African Americans. He continued his brilliant and colorful career in boxing until his retirement in 1981. Although today Muhammad Ali suffers from Parkinson's disease, he is still considered one of America's greatest athletes, and was chosen to light the Olympic torch at the opening ceremonies of the 1996 summer Olympics in Atlanta, Georgia.

Still a beloved public figure, Muhammad Ali lights the Olympic flame at the 1996 summer games in Atlanta, Georgia.

Philbert X (left) denounces his "wayward brother Malcolm" in this photo taken at a press conference in Chicago, Illinois, on March 26, 1964.

Worse than that, Malcolm's life was in danger. One of Malcolm's former trusted deputies in New York had told other members, "If you knew what the minister did, you'd go out and kill him yourself." Malcolm knew that to a loyal member of the Nation of Islam, that statement was practically an order to kill him.

Then Langston X, a former assistant of Malcolm's, informed him that the order had actually been issued. He had been instructed to wire Malcolm's car to blow up. Langston, though, decided to disobey. Nevertheless, there were many more Muslim brothers who believed that Malcolm deserved death, and they would obey without question.

Although deeply shaken by the violent reactions against him in the Nation of Islam, Malcolm still believed in his mission. He had not lost his faith, and he was convinced he was meant to lead black Americans, especially the poor people in the ghettos. At a press conference in March 1964, he announced that he was no longer part of the Nation of Islam. However, he refused to criticize Elijah Muhammad or the Nation of Islam. He said that he was forming a new black Muslim organization, the Muslim Mosque, Inc.

A Pilgrimage to Mecca

Before he plunged into this new enterprise, Malcolm decided this was the time for him to make a pilgrimage to Mecca. Every faithful Muslim is supposed to visit the holiest city of Islam at least once in a lifetime, if at all possible. Ever since Malcolm converted to Islam, he had thought of making the trip to Mecca.

Malcolm's religion was very important to him, and he had been troubled for years by some of the odd teachings of the Nation of Islam. He knew from his readings and from conversations with orthodox Muslims that the worldwide religion of Islam could not regard Elijah Muhammad as a divine being. To traditional Muslims, many of Muhammad's teachings were farfetched, including his claim that the whole white race was the result of a genetic experiment by a black scientist, and the myth that there was a spaceship orbiting Earth, filled with bombs for the battle of Armageddon.

Malcolm's sister Ella heartily supported his plans for a pilgrimage. She had left the Nation of Islam in 1959, but she was a faithful Muslim. She had started a school and day-care center for Muslim children in Boston. Although she had been planning a pilgrimage to Mecca herself, Ella gladly gave Malcolm the money to go instead. In April 1964, Malcolm boarded a plane for Cairo, Egypt.

On his trip to Egypt, Malcolm saw the Great Sphinx at Giza, which is believed to represent the face of the pharaoh Khafre. The Great Sphinx and the Khafre pyramid were built more than 4,500 years ago.

Mecca

In the religion of Islam, the city of Mecca, in Saudi Arabia, near the Red Sea, is the holiest place. It is the birthplace of the prophet Muhammad, the founder of Islam. In the center of the city is the Sacred Mosque, the holiest mosque in the Muslim world, containing the cubical shrine called the Kaaba.

Muslim pilgrims circle the Kaaba in this 1996 photo. The traditional ritual is to circle the Kaaba three times clockwise, quickly, and then four times counterclockwise, more slowly.

Every year, millions of pilgrims from around the world visit Mecca. They must all wear the same pilgrim's clothing, the *ihram*, consisting of two plain white sheets. The simple clothing symbolizes that all people are equal in the sight of Allah. While they wear the *ihram*, the pilgrims must not shave, cut their nails, or wear jewelry.

In Mecca, the pilgrims perform ritual acts to commemorate events in the lives of the prophet Abraham (Ibrahim) and his servant girl Hagar (Hajar), who was left in the desert to die. Pilgrims walk around the Kaaba, said to have been built by Abraham, seven times. They walk back and forth between the hills of Safa and Marwah seven times. Most pilgrims also drink from the Zamzam Well that saved Hagar from dying of thirst in the wilderness.

In Egypt, Malcolm was thrilled to see the Sphinx and the pyramids. These were world-famous symbols of ancient Egypt, which Malcolm believed had been a civilization of black people.

In Mecca, Malcolm was deeply moved to find himself accepted as a Muslim—one of tens of thousands of other pilgrims. He had never experienced brotherhood like this. "In my thirty-nine years on Earth," he wrote to Betty and Ella, "the Holy City of Mecca had been the first time I had ever stood before the Creator of All and felt like a complete human being."

In Mecca, Malcolm was deeply moved to find himself accepted as a Muslim—one of tens of thousands of other pilgrims.

Malcolm described in letters how he was "speechless and spellbound" to be worshipping with Muslims "of all colors, from blue-eyed blonds to black-skinned Africans." There was a "spirit of unity and brotherhood that my experiences in America had led me to believe never could exist between the white and the non-white." It was a life-changing experience. Malcolm had to rethink his beliefs about white people. Maybe there was even hope for white Americans.

Before returning home, Malcolm traveled on to Africa. He visited Ghana, where he was received by President Nkrumah, and several other independent African nations. Malcolm was excited by the idea of Pan-Africanism, the movement to unite all native African peoples. Malcolm had sometimes thought that Marcus Garvey, his parents' hero, was right. Garvey had urged American blacks to leave the United States and establish their own nation in Africa. Because that wasn't practical, it was important for African Americans to know that they weren't just a minority population in the United States. They belonged to the vast, worldwide group of people of African descent.

A Change of Heart

When he returned to the United States in May 1964, Malcolm gave statements to the media about his change of heart.

His pilgrimage to Mecca had such a deep effect on him that he began signing letters as "El Hajj Malik El-Shabazz." "El Hajj" is the title given to a person who has made the hajj, or pilgrimage. "Malik" is an Arabic name, while "Shabazz," according to Elijah Muhammad, was the tribal name of the original black people. Malcolm now intended to cooperate with other organizations fighting for black rights, including civil rights groups.

While Malcolm believed more deeply in Islam than ever, he wanted to downplay religion in his public mission. He wanted to join forces with the civil rights movement he had criticized so bitterly. He announced the founding of the Organization of Afro-American Unity, to coordinate all the groups working for black people's rights.

Now that Malcolm was outside the Nation of Islam, he was free to acknowledge that he and Martin Luther King were working toward the same goal. He also felt sure that they would both die for their cause. It was anybody's guess, he thought, as to which of them would be **martyred** first.

About four years before the assassination of Martin Luther King, Jr., Malcolm X and King were photographed during their first and only meeting on March 26, 1964. They were both in Washington to attend the Senate debate of the Civil Rights Bill.

CHAPTER 14

A "Black Shining Prince"

"I present to you one who is willing to put himself on the line for you, a man who would give his life for you."

—Benjamin X, introducing Malcolm X

O f the nationally known black leaders, Malcolm X was the one who was most in touch with the people living in poverty and crime-ridden ghettos. He had grown up in that setting himself. Once, an interviewer commented to Malcolm that most members of the Nation of Islam were from the low-income group. "Most *black people* in the United States," Malcolm replied dryly, "are in the low-income group."

Malcolm was well aware of the unrest seething in the ghettos of northern cities. Before he left on his trip to Mecca in April, he had predicted that the summer of 1964 would be a "long, hot summer." In fact, there was a riot in Harlem that July, over the shooting of a black teenager by the police. Uprisings broke out in the black ghettos of other cities as well.

Growing Danger

During this time, Malcolm continued to work on his autobiography with Alex Haley. He talked wistfully to Haley about what he would like to do if his life wasn't consumed with fighting for his race. He wished he could go back to school and learn other languages: Arabic, Swahili, Chinese. He wished he could study for a law degree as he had hoped when he was a young teenager.

However, Malcolm felt sure that he wouldn't live much longer. The Nation of Islam was in turmoil, and they blamed Malcolm. With Malcolm's encouragement, two of the young women who had given birth to Elijah Muhammad's children out of wedlock, took Muhammad to court. They wanted to force him to provide financial support for their children.

The Nation of Islam was in turmoil, and they blamed Malcolm.

At the beginning of June 1964, Malcolm stated on national television that Elijah Muhammad had fathered six children out of wedlock. He added that the Nation of Islam would kill to keep this truth from coming out. Throughout the country, many Nation of Islam mosques lost members. Even one of Muhammad's adult sons, Wallace Muhammad, publicly accused his father of being corrupt and power hungry, as did an adult grandson, Hasan Sharrieff.

There were many NOI young men who thought it was Allah's will for them to kill Malcolm X, their former leader. Malcolm also speculated that he might be killed by white racists, or even by black integrationists who thought he was harming the civil rights movement.

Fire Again

In the dark early morning of February 14, 1965, Malcolm, Betty, and their children were asleep at home. They had four daughters now, including the six-week-old baby, Gamilah. Malcolm had just returned from another long trip, this time to England and France, and he was exhausted. About two thirty in the morning, they were awakened by the crash of breaking glass. Smoke and flames burst out, and Malcolm just managed to hustle his pregnant wife and their four young daughters out the back door to safety.

Someone had firebombed the house through the big front window. To Malcolm's outrage, a Nation of Islam spokesman suggested that Malcolm had caused the fire himself— perhaps for the publicity.

Malcolm X is photographed on February 15, 1965, getting out of his car in front of his firebombed house in Queens, New York.

For the next few days, Malcolm, Betty, and the children stayed with friends. On the night of February 20, Malcolm moved to a hotel, because he was worried that his presence was putting his family in danger. The next day he was scheduled to speak for his Organization of African-American Unity at the Audubon Ballroom in Harlem.

The Assassination

On the afternoon of February 21, 1965, Malcolm's assistant Benjamin X introduced him to the audience. "I present to you one who is willing to put himself on the line for you, a man who would give his life for you," he said.

Betty and the girls watched from the front row as Malcolm stepped up to the podium. The audience stood up, applauding loudly. Malcolm greeted them, "Asalaikum, brothers and sisters!"

The audience returned the greeting. Before Malcolm could begin his speech, there was a scuffle in the crowd. A smoke bomb went off, causing the audience to scream and jump up. Malcolm tried to speak a few calming words. In the confusion, three men ran toward the stage, firing their guns.

Malcolm was struck by sixteen bullets. He was rushed to the hospital, and attempts were made to revive him. But as Betty— who was trained as a nurse—already knew, Malcolm was dead. He was only thirty-nine years old.

A few days later, at a Nation of Islam convention in Chicago, Elijah Muhammad spoke fervently about Malcolm X. He had to stop often, overcome with emotion and fits of coughing. "We didn't want to kill Malcolm and didn't try to kill him. . . . His foolish teaching brought him to his own end."

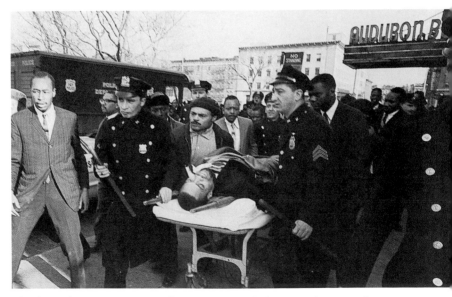

After being shot sixteen times on February 21, 1965, Malcolm is carried on a stretcher from the Audubon Ballroom. He is declared dead at Columbia Presbyterian Hospital at 3:30 p.m.

Although three men belonging to the Nation of Islam were arrested, tried, and convicted of shooting Malcolm X, there was some doubt as to whether authorities had arrested the right men.

Malcolm was hated by many different groups, from the Nation of Islam to the Ku Klux Klan. Malcolm himself hinted to *Life* magazine photographer Gordon Parks and to his biographer, Alex Haley, that the CIA was after him. Certainly the CIA and the FBI considered Malcolm a dangerous man, and so did the New York Police Department.

The most likely conclusion seemed to be the obvious one: He was killed by members of the Nation of Islam—men who thought he deserved death for betraying Elijah Muhammad.

The Funeral

Two days after the shooting, mourners stood in line for hours outside the funeral home in Harlem. They filed past Malcolm X's coffin to pay their respects. In all, twenty-two thousand people viewed the body.

Thousands more gathered outside the church where the funeral took place on Saturday. To the fifteen hundred people inside, the actor Ossie Davis spoke eloquently about his friend. "Malcolm was our manhood, our living, black manhood! This was his meaning to his people. And in honoring him, we honor the best in ourselves." Malcolm was, Davis declared, "a Prince— our own black shining Prince!—who didn't hesitate to die, because he loved us so."

Martin Luther King, Jr., sent Betty Shabazz a condolence telegram, which read: "I always had a deep affection for Malcolm and felt that he had a great ability to put his finger on the existence and the root of the problem." Three years later, King himself would be assassinated.

The Nation of Islam After Malcolm

After Elijah Muhammad's death in 1975, his son Wallace Muhammad was appointed head of the Nation of Islam. He tried to bring the NOI in line with mainstream Islam, and he finally disbanded the organization. Then Louis Farrakhan, who had taken leadership of the mosque in New York after Malcolm's assassination, decided to reorganize and restore the Nation of Islam as Elijah Muhammad had originally intended it. Under Louis Farrakhan, the Nation of Islam rebounded, and in 1995 they organized the "Million Man March" on the Mall in Washington, D.C., to show black solidarity. There was no clear count on whether there were a million men marching that day.

The Million Man March on October 16, 1995, was conceived by NOI leader Louis Farrakhan. This event for African American men included voter registration and encouraging volunteer work in black communities.

At the time of Malcolm's assassination, Betty was pregnant with twins—two more daughters. They were born that September. Malcolm's autobiography was also published that year—now dedicated to Betty and to their children, rather than to Elijah Muhammad. The *Autobiography of Malcolm X* became a best seller, and is now considered a classic on the black American experience.

The Legacy of Malcolm X

In his short life, Malcolm X changed the way many black people thought about themselves. He empowered African Americans—especially those who were poor and powerless. He told them they didn't have to wait for kindly white people to help them. Blacks could help each other now to escape poverty. Blacks could demand political power, and get it.

Malcolm bolstered black Americans' pride—telling them they should be proud to be black. He encouraged them to drop the terms *Negro* and *colored* and to refer to themselves as *black* and *African American*. Many black people began to give their children African names, to wear traditional African clothing, and, starting in 1966, to celebrate the African American holiday of Kwanzaa.

Malcolm also changed the way white people thought about blacks, especially when they saw him—an intelligent, proud black leader, standing as erect as a king and fearless as a warrior. He made them understand that African Americans were not contented with their lot. Statements like "Freedom by any means necessary" made white Americans realize that everyone had to work for equality and justice in order to avoid violence.

Malcolm helped change the way history is taught in American public schools. The achievements of black cultures in Africa, the brutal history of American slavery, and the extraordinary accomplishments of many black Americans are now standard units of study in today's school curriculum.

Through Malcolm's devotion to his faith, many black Americans were introduced to Islam. Of the orthodox Muslims in the United States today, about 1.5 million are black.

Countless people have been inspired by Malcolm's personal story—a self-destructive youth transformed into an educated leader who positively influenced thousands of black people and made important contributions to society. One of the many people influenced by Malcolm X is the movie director Spike Lee. He thought the *Autobiography of Malcolm X* was the most important book he would ever read. "It changed the way I thought; it changed the way I acted. It has given me courage that I didn't know I had inside me. I'm one of hundreds of thousands whose life was changed for the better."

Malcolm X smiles in this photograph taken February 16, 1965, in Rochester, New York. His public words were often harsh, but in person he could be warm and charming.

Glossary

black nationalist—a person who believes that African Americans should support each other and become independent from white society.

brainwashed—having undergone an intensive, forcible process to destroy a person's basic convictions and attitudes and replace them with another set of fixed beliefs.

civil rights—the rights belonging to every U.S. citizen, including equal protection under the law, freedom of speech and religion, and freedom from discrimination.

colonialism—a policy by which a nation controls foreign peoples dependent upon it.

conscientious objector—a person who refuses to serve in the military because of religious or moral beliefs.

demagogue—a leader who gains power by stirring up his listeners' emotions.

foster home—a home where volunteers provide care for children.

ghettos—the sections of a city in which a minority group is concentrated. These areas are usually densely populated and run down.

hypocrisy—pretending to believe one thing while actually doing another.

integration—bringing people of different racial groups together in equal association.

lynched—executed, usually by hanging, without due process of law.

martyred—killed because of one's devotion to his or her beliefs.

racial discrimination—showing preference or prejudice based solely on a person's race.

racist—a person showing some form of prejudice based on a person's race.

Reconstruction—the period after the Civil War (1865–1877) when the former Confederate states were controlled by the federal government, before they were readmitted to the Union.

segregated—to be kept apart by race, for reasons of prejudice.

stereotype—a conventional, oversimplified image.

supremacist—a person who believes that a particular group is or should be dominant in power and authority.

welfare agency—a government service that distributes aid for people in need.

Bibliography

Books

Breitman, George, ed. *By Any Means Necessary: Speeches, Interviews and a Letter by Malcolm X.* New York: Pathfinder Press, Inc., 1970.

Carson, Clayborne; David J. Garrow, Gerald Gill, Vincent Harding; Darlene Clark Hine, eds. *The Eyes on the Prize Civil Rights Reader: Documents, Speeches, and Firsthand Accounts from the Black Freedom Struggle, 1954-1990.* New York: Viking Penguin, 1991.

Clarke, John Henrik. *Malcolm X: The Man and His Times.* New York: Macmillan, 1969.

Collins, Rodnell P., with A. Peter Bailey. *Seventh Child: A Family Memoir of Malcolm X.* Secaucus, New Jersey: Birch Lane Press, 1998.

Cone, James H. *Martin & Malcolm & America: a Dream or a Nightmare.* Maryknoll, New York: Orbis Books, 1991.

Dodson, Howard; Christopher Moore; and Roberta Yancy. *The Black New Yorkers: The Schomburg Illustrated Chronology.* New York: John Wiley & Sons, 2000.

Lincoln, C. Eric. *The Black Muslims in America, 3rd edition.* Grand Rapids, Michigan: Wm. B. Eerdmans Publishing Company, and Trenton, New Jersey: Africa World Press, Inc., 1994.

Perry, Bruce. *Malcolm: The Life of a Man Who Changed Black America.* Barrytown, New York: Station Hill Press, 1991.

Rickford, Russell John. *Betty Shabazz: A Remarkable Story of Survival and Faith Before and After Malcolm X.* Naperville, Illinois: Sourcebooks, 2003.

Shabazz, Ilyasah. *Growing Up X.* New York: Ballantine Publishing Group, 2002.

X, Malcolm, as told to Alex Haley. *The Autobiography of Malcolm X.* New York: Random House, 1965.

Films

Malcolm X. Directed by Spike Lee, starring Denzel Washington, based closely on Malcolm X's autobiography, 1992.

Malcolm X. 1972 documentary, distributed by Warner Bros., with video footage of Malcolm's speeches and interviews.

Malcolm X: Make It Plain. PBS Documentary in The American Experience series, 2005.

Web Sites

Federal Bureau of Investigation files on Malcolm Little, released under the Freedom of Information Act.
   http://foia.fbi.gov/malcolmx/malcolmx1.pdf

The Malcolm X Project at Columbia University
   http://www.columbia.edu/cu/ccbh/mxp/initiatives.html

The Official Web Site of Malcolm X
   http://www.cmgworldwide.com/historic/malcolm/home.php

Image Credits

About the Author

Beatrice Gormley is the author of many biographies and novels for young readers. She lives with her husband, Robert Gormley, in Massachusetts. For more information about Beatrice and her books, visit www.beatricegormley.com.

Index